Introduction

North Wales has some of the mo[st] and a fascinating maritime and [...] is the new Wales Coast Path, a [...] from near Chester around the full c[oast ...] Welsh Assembly Government and laun[ched ...] Wales the Coast Path runs along a coa[st ...] Heritage status, while on Anglesey and the Llŷn peninsula much falls within designated Areas of Outstanding Natural Beauty, some owned by the National Trust. The coastal landscape includes sand dunes, cliffs, tidal river estuaries, sand and shingle beaches, sheltered coves and harbours, the stunning limestone headlands of the Great and Little Orme and the foothills of the Carneddau mountains overlooking the sea. From the saltmarsh and extensive mudflats of Traeth Lafan to the high rocky cliffs of Holyhead Mountain, the coast provides an important habitat of international importance for many species of birds. It also contains important historical sites, impressive ancient monuments and buildings, as well as 19thC navigational aids for shipping.

From the Dee Estuary west to Anglesey and the Llŷn peninsula the coast offers many great coastal walks. In this book I have selected 30 walks which reflect the coast's rich diversity, scenic value, historic interest, and some of the best sections of the Coast Path. They pass through historic ports, popular seaside resorts, and the medieval fortified town of Conwy, a World Heritage Site. They visit nature reserves, a Heritage Park, remote ancient churches, holy wells, Iron Age hillforts, a Neolithic burial chamber and a small romantic island. They feature marinas, lighthouses, maritime beacons, an old telegraph station and stunning views.

The routes, which range from a 1¾ mile dune and beach walk to an 8 mile walk along the unspoilt cliffs of northern Llŷn, are well within the capabilities of most people. Many routes contain shorter walk options. They follow public rights of way or permissive paths, and occasionally cross Open Access land. Walking boots are recommended, along with appropriate clothing to protect against the elements. Please remember that the condition of the paths can vary according to season and weather! Contact the local Highways Authority regarding any problems encountered.

Each walk has a detailed map and description which enables the route to be followed without difficulty, but be aware that changes in detail can occur at any time. The location of each walk is shown on the back cover and a summary of the key characteristics of each is provided on the inside covers. This includes an estimated walking time, but allow longer to enjoy the scenery. For more coastal walks consider other books in the Kittiwake series.

Please observe The Country Code and respect any ancient site visited. *Enjoy your walking!*

G*reenfield Valley*, near to sources of lead and other ores, and with easy access by sea to Liverpool, developed rapidly during the 18thC as an important industrial centre, regarded as the cradle of the Industrial Revolution in North Wales. Its constant flow of water – 4,000 gallons a minute – which never froze, provided the power for a line of mills and factories that stretched down the narrow valley. It steadily declined during the 19thC with the development of steam power, and the need for larger sites and better port facilities.

1 Go along the High Street and at its end turn RIGHT. Cross the inner ring road and go down steps then Well Street. Continue down past the graveyard to St. James church and St Winefride's chapel, then down the B5121 to the entrance of St Winefride's Well (**A**) *(open daily)*. *Enclosed in an early 16thC chapel, the famous well chamber with bath, renowned for its healing properties, has attracted pilgrims for many centuries.* Continue past the Art & Craft Mill/Tea rooms. Just before commercial premises turn RIGHT and follow the signposted path up to a kissing gate, then its waymarked left fork alongside a wall and past seats.

2 Just before a large finger post, turn LEFT down a stepped path. Turn RIGHT through an iron archway and go along a path, soon alongside Battery Pool. Turn RIGHT across the dam above the site of Greenfield Mills (**B**). *Established in 1776, the Battery Works produced brass pots and pans, which were sent via Liverpool to Africa and exchanged for slaves.* Continue up past a chimney through trees to join the track bed of the former Holywell branch railway – *the steepest passenger railway in Great Britain.* Follow it LEFT down the wooded valley past waymarked side paths. At a staggered junction of paths, turn LEFT down a stepped path, past the nearby dam of a former mill pool and through Meadow Mill site (**C**) – *which made rollers for printing patterns on cloth and copper sheets.* Continue past the large Flour Mill pool then follow a narrow lane past the Lower Cotton Mill (**D**) – *used between 1785-1840 for spinning cotton brought from the Americas* – then the former Abbey Wire Mill (**E**).

3 When it bends left continue between buildings and past the Farm Museum (**F**). Just to the west is a mill pool (**G**) – *all that remains of the important Parys Mine Company copper works built in 1787, which produced copper fittings and sheathing for wooden sailing ships.* With a café ahead turn RIGHT past the Visitor Centre and on past Basingwerk Abbey [1132–1536] (**H**), then down to the large car park by the A548. Follow the pavement opposite LEFT, then turn RIGHT along Dock Road. Follow

WALK 1

HOLYWELL TO BAGILLT

DESCRIPTION A 5¼ mile linear walk, linked to a regular bus service, featuring a newly created section of the Coast Path along the Dee estuary and the area's fascinating industrial and maritime past. The route descends to famous St Winefride's Well, which gave the town its name, then explores Greenfield Valley Heritage Park, containing 12thC Basingwerk Abbey and the remains of 18thC mills, factories and mill pools. From historic Greenfield Dock it follows the Coast Path to the new Bettisfield recreational site, near Bagillt. Allow about 3 hours. From the car park by the Stag Inn in the centre of Bagillt turn left to a bus stop to catch the Arriva 11 bus to Holywell centre

START Holywell High Street [SJ 185759].

it over the railway line, then past the end of Greenfield Dock – *once a busy port, with up to 40 ships trading in raw materials and finished products from industries in the Greenfield Valley. Short lived ferry services also ran from here in the 19thC.*

4 Pass under a barrier gate and follow the signposted Bettisfield/Bagillt/Coast Path along the eastern side of the Dock, then across open ground and past an industrial estate. After crossing a narrow creek the gated Coast Path continues on an embankment along the edge of the saltmarsh, then crosses an old industrial site to a kissing gate just before the railway line at the head of Dee Bank Gutter (**J**). *This small port was once linked to nearby leadworks and a foundry. Briefly in the early 19thC passenger services to Liverpool via Parkgate and Hoylake operated*

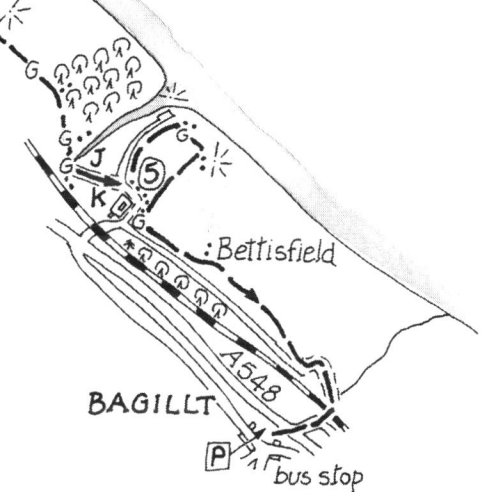

from here. It is known locally as 'The Holy' from the daily average of 23 million gallons of water which gushes from the outlet of the Milwr tunnel, which originally shared the same source as St Winefride's Holy Well. The 10 mile tunnel was driven inland from here in stages between 1897–1957, primarily to drain lead mines in Holywell and Halkyn Mountain. Continue along an access road to a barrier gate by the corner of a high fence compound, containing the former winding house of Bettisfield Colliery (1872–1934), now a cars spares site (**K**). Cross to a path opposite beneath a sign welcoming you to 'Bettisfield – Gateway to the Dee'.

5 Follow it LEFT beside the road to a car park overlooking an inlet containing small fishing boats. The estuary path is currently closed, so go through a kissing gate on the right and up onto the main Bettisfield site to an information board at a great viewpoint along the estuary. Now follow a wide path down to a kissing gate opposite the car spares compound. Just beyond bend LEFT past wooden sculptures, a nearby car park and lane. The waymarked Coast Path continues along the edge of the saltmarsh then follows the lane/stony track to a footbridge over the railway at the former Bagillt Station (1849–1965). *The nearby creek, now silted, was once an important cargo port handling large amounts of coal, lead, zinc and copper.* Cross the footbridge and go along Station Road ahead. Cross the dual carriageway with care and follow a path to the car park.

WALK 2
TALACRE

DESCRIPTION Two short walks near the mouth of the Dee Estuary. A 1¾ mile walk (**A**) featuring dunes, beach and a 19thC lighthouse. A 1½ mile walk (**B**) near Point of Ayr Nature Reserve, an important roosting site for wetland birds, to an RSPB hide. *Bring binoculars.* Allow about 1 hour.

START Car park by the Smuggler's Inn, Talacre [SJ 124848].

DIRECTIONS From the A548 follow the road into Talacre to the car park and inn just before its end.

*G**ronant Dunes and Talacre Warren SSSI is rich in plant, animal, bird and insect life. The land owned by BHP Billiton, which processes gas piped from platforms visible in Liverpool Bay, is managed with other agencies for nature conservation. A notable landmark is the lighthouse, built in 1819 to replace an earlier 1777 one. It had a flashing light with a range of 19 miles. It has survived a replacement 1844 iron tower, and a later tower built in 1891. Its subsequent uses have included a store, wartime lookout, and holiday home.*

Walk A Go to the road end, then take a cycle/walkway on the left signposted to Gronant into Gronant Dunes and Talacre Warren SSSI. Follow the wide surfaced recreational route for nearly ½ mile, then turn RIGHT on a concrete path signposted to the beach. Follow the waymarked permissive bridleway through the dunes onto the beach, or alternative waymarked black trail high tide option as shown. Head east past the lighthouse and a large finger post to leave the beach by a flagpole. Go across to a viewing platform on dunes ahead, past information boards, and along the embanked path to the road end.

Walk B Go to the road end and up to the Talacre Beach information board. Follow the path signposted to Ffynnongroyw/Bird Hide along the embankment, later passing the perimeter of BHP gas terminal, then bending left to the hide. Retrace your steps.

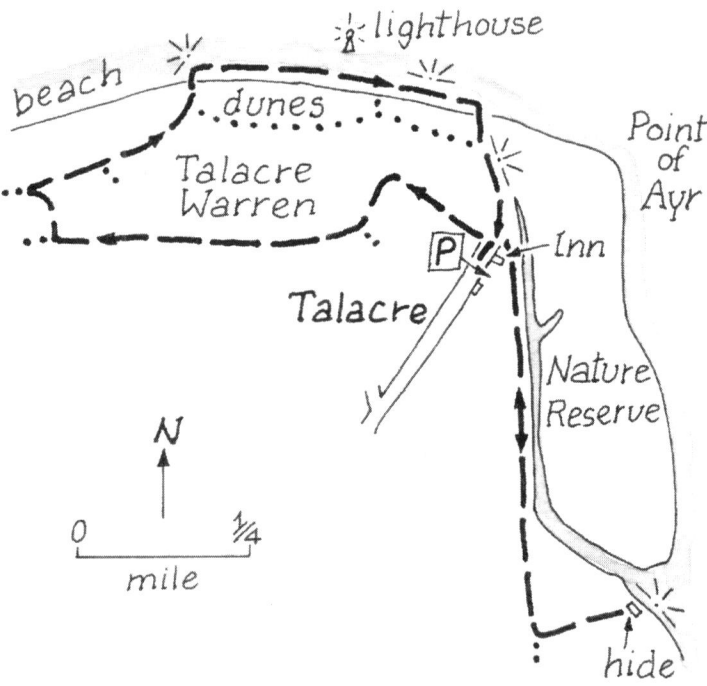

WALKS 2 & 3

WALK 3
GRONANT DUNES

DESCRIPTION A 2¾ mile walk through Gronant Dunes, a designated Local Nature Reserve and Special Site of Scientific Interest. The dunes, extending east from a single narrow ridge into a series of parallel ridges, support a range of insects and plants, including the dominant marram grass, and less common species such as sea-holly, pyramidal orchid, sea and portland spurge. The foreshore and shingle attract a variety of birds, including wintering waders, cormorants and the largest breeding colony of little terns in Wales. Allow about 1½ hours.
START Barkby Beach car park, Prestatyn. [SJ 068840].
DIRECTIONS On the eastern outskirts of Prestatyn, turn off the A548 coast road into Marine Road East, signposted to Barkby beach. Go past Pontins, and on the bend enter the beach car park by Prestatyn Sailing Club.

1 From the car park follow the signposted Wales Coast Path east along a short section of promenade, then along a rough path above the stony beach by Gronant Dunes. Take the next but one signposted path up a wooden walkway to the top of the dunes. Here turn LEFT and follow the waymarked Wales Coast Path along the top of the dunes and past the fence corner. At the next waymark post turn LEFT, then follow the path along the edge of the dunes, past another waymark post and on through the middle of the expansive dunes ahead, later becoming more enclosed. *En route, visible on the nearby hills above Gronant is the white house of Foel Nant – the former Voelnant Telegraph Station, dating from 1841.* After ¾ mile with a small shallow lake ahead (dry sometimes) you reach a signposted path junction. Turn LEFT and follow the boardwalked path across the dunes to the signposted viewing platform overlooking Gronant Beach – *providing an opportunity to observe the little tern colony (do not disturb) and enjoy coastal views.* Return to the finger post then continue on the path signposted to Presthaven to pass along the southern edge of the lake.

2 Shortly, turn RIGHT on the signposted path. Follow the embanked path for about 15 yards to an information board about 'Endangered Predators'. Here turn sharp RIGHT down a path and on past two small fenced ponds. At the rear of another similar information board, follow a path LEFT to a nearby old board. Turn RIGHT and follow a path past an old fence, then alongside the wooden perimeter fence of the golf course. The path then continues along the edge of the dunes overlooking the golf course and on – *with good views ahead of the mountains of Snowdonia and the Little Orme* – to join your outward route.

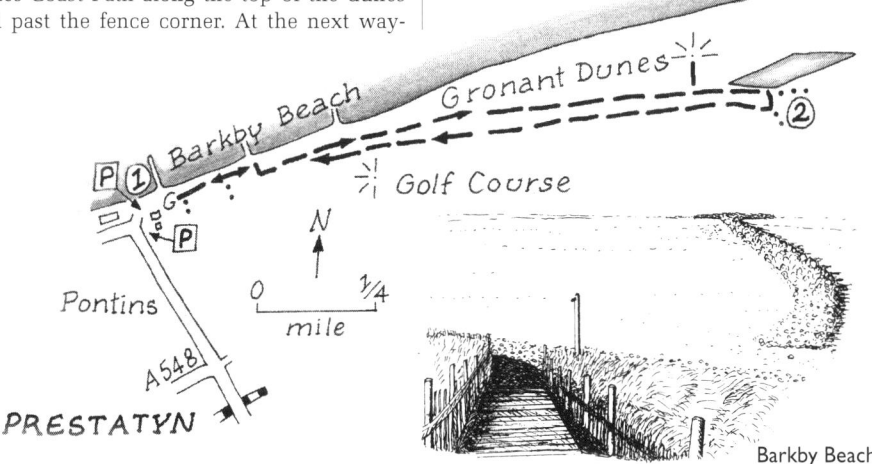

Barkby Beach

3 Go past its small harbour – *created in the 1980s when the breakwater was built to prevent local flooding* – then follow the lower cycle/walkway above the rocky shore to St Trillo's Chapel. *This tiny church stands on an ancient healing well, where the 6thC Celtic saint built his cell.* Continue along the wide promenade. Shortly join the nearby road then continue on a raised walkway beside the sea-wall – *enjoying a good view to Llandrillo Church with Bryn Euryn beyond, and to the Carneddau mountains.* Go past the golf club – *where the first aeroplane landed in North Wales in 1910.* At the end of the sea-wall continue above the shore by iron railings.

4 About 30 yards before houses, descend steps on the waymarked North Wales Path and continue along the edge of the beach beneath gardens, then follow the NWP up steps then along a road through a housing estate. At its end go up steps to an information board on the Little Orme. (For **route B** turn left along the wide stony path. When it splits, keep ahead to a hidden kissing gate, then go up a lane. Just past the second house, go through a kissing gate on the right. Follow the path through trees, keeping with the left fork up the wood edge, then follow the enclosed path to a farm. Follow its access lane to the B5115. Turn right. to point **6**.)

5 For **route a** Turn RIGHT along the wide stony path to reach a finger post near an old quarry incline. Continue ahead for a good view of the cliffs with nesting birds and a small inlet, then return to follow the NWP

I For **Walk A** continue along Abergele Road, then go down Beach Road. Shortly, cross a small bridge on the right over a stream. Continue beside the stream through Tan-y-Coed gardens to a road. *The gardens were created in the late 19thC by Sir Charles Woodall, a shipping magnate, who lived in a nearby mansion, now demolished. He built the castellated stone folly in 1894 as a retreat for smoking his pipe in the last years of his life!* Pass under the A55 and railway bridges to reach the promenade. Follow it west to the road leading up into Eirias Park at point **2**.

For **Walk B** follow the road through Eirias Park past the school to its end by the Leisure Centre. *The 47 acres of Eirias Park have provided leisure and recreation for the public since 1923. Its boating lake opened in 1935.* Follow a path down past the bowling green, then a road down to reach the promenade.

2 Head along the promenade towards Colwyn pier. *The pier opened in 1900 and was extended in 1903 to 750 feet long. The current pavilion was built in 1934 in Art Deco style. The pier has had a chequered history, with fire destroying two earlier pavilions, and is now in poor condition. After public support against its demolition there are hopes that funds can be found towards its eventual restoration.* Continue along the promenade to the Tourist Information Point and clock tower opposite the Cayley Arms in Rhos-on-Sea.

WALK 4

OLD COLWYN TO LLANDUDNO

DESCRIPTION A 7¾ mile (**A**) coastal or 7¼ mile (**B**) linear walk, offering extensive coastal views, following a section of the Wales Coast Path/North Wales Path from Old Colwyn or Colwyn Bay to Llandudno, linked to frequent bus services – visit: www.conwy.gov.uk/publictransport. After a short walk through Eirias Park or Tan y Coed gardens respectively the route heads along the promenade past Colwyn Pier to Rhos-on-Sea. After visiting the ancient St Trillo's Chapel it continues above the shore to Penrhyn Bay. After a short section of beach and a climb across the Little Orme (**route a**) or a lower alternative (**route b**) it descends to Craigside and follows the majestic promenade along Llandudno Bay. Allow about 4½ hours. The route can easily be undertaken as shorter walks linked to the same bus services.

START Abergele Road, Old Colwyn [SH 867783] or Eirias Park entrance, Colwyn Bay [SH 856782].

DIRECTIONS First take the no. 12 (Rhyl) 14 or 15 (Llysfaen) bus from stop D in Mostyn Street, Llandudno centre to Colwyn Bay. Alight at Eirias Park for Walk B or The Royal College of Nursing building opposite The Plough in Abergele Road, Old Colwyn for Walk A.

up the incline to a stile at the top. Turn sharp LEFT and follow the waymarked path to a good viewpoint and up the hillside to join a fence. At its corner the path turns LEFT and rises through gorse. At a waymark post, where it levels out, ignore a path bending right but keep ahead to a kissing gate to enter Rhiwledyn Nature Reserve. Follow the path down to the road.

6 Go along the pavement towards the Great Orme, descending past Craigside Manor and Premier Inn. At the last house descend onto the grassy foreshore and continue to a paddling pool, cafe and toilets. Now simply follow the wide promenade along Llandudno's North Shore – *created along with the elegant buildings to provide a classical frontage to the new resort* – to the Cenotaph near its end.

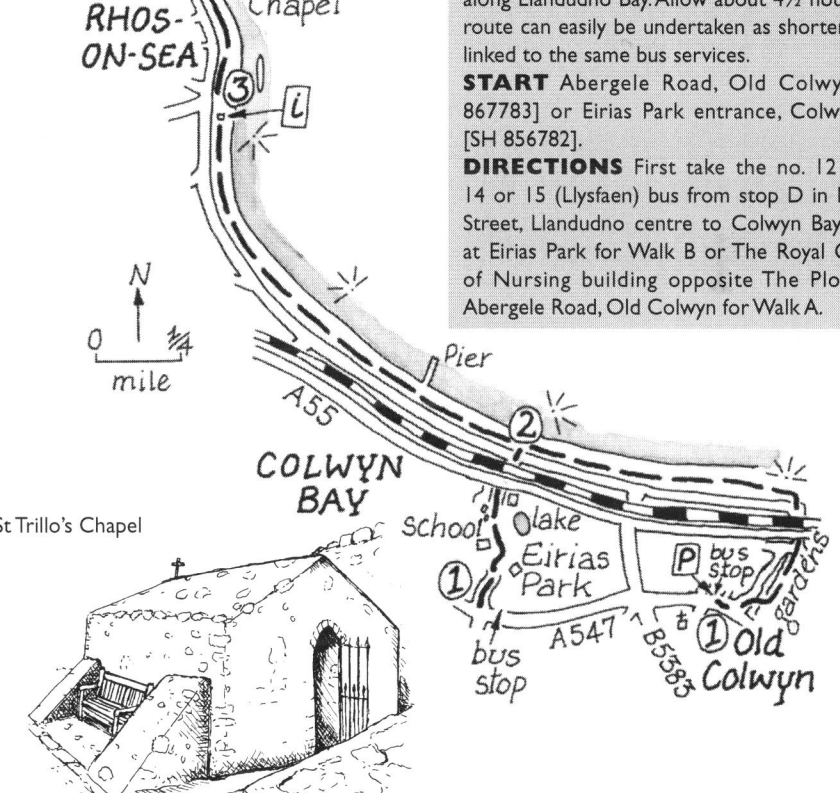

St Trillo's Chapel

WALK 5
AROUND THE GREAT ORME

DESCRIPTION A 5½ mile walk around this dramatic limestone headland, offering close views of its stunning cliff scenery and birdlife. The route first follows Marine Drive up to Pen-y-Gogarth (Great Orme's Head), with its vertical cliffs, former lighthouse and café. After a long steady descent, enjoying panoramic sea and mountain views, the route returns across the limestone hillside and through Haulfre Gardens (tea-rooms). Allow about 3 hours.
START Cenotaph, northern end of the North Shore Promenade, Llandudno [SH 782826].

Marine Drive is a spectacular one-way toll road around the Great Orme which opened in 1878, to replace an 1858 path, which Prime Minister William Gladstone complained about during a visit in 1868. The Great Orme's scenery is best appreciated leisurely on foot from Marine Drive's pavement. You may see the famous feral Kashmir goats, said to originate from a pair sent with others from India as a present for Queen Victoria, which have been roaming wild here since the 1890s. The name 'Orme' is said to derive from a Viking name for 'sea monster' – an apt description when viewed from sea!

1 Go along the promenade, then follow the walkway behind the Grand Hotel (1901) to the iron pier (1876/7). Turn through its gated entrance then walk along the pavement overlooking the rocky shore past Happy Valley Gardens to reach the castellated toll house at the start of Marine Drive. Continue beneath the limestone cliffs at the eastern tip of the Great Orme – *a nesting site for seabirds and containing arches, formed by stone extraction.* Shortly the road heads west, passes a side road, then rises steadily between limestone crags and steep cliffs – *with a view ahead of the former Great Orme's Head lighthouse (1862-1985)* – to eventually reach the Rest and Be Thankful Café. Shortly after passing Ffynnon Gaseg the road descends south-east – *offering extensive views to Anglesey and the Carneddau mountains.* Below is an area known as the Gunsite, a former military training site. Eventually you reach another castellated toll house.

2 Go through a kissing gate near it, then follow the path ahead, soon bending up and continuing across the limestone hillside past seats. *Known as the Invalids or Lovers Walk, it has been a popular pathway since Victorian times, offering panoramic views across Llandudno.* After a gate continue through Haulfre Gardens, soon passing Haulfre Tea-rooms and toilets. Go down Cwlach Road and along the narrow road ahead to reach Old Road with its tram line. Follow it down to crossroads just below the Tram Station. *The cable tram to the summit opened in 1902/3.* Turn left along Church Walks and continue to the promenade.

WALK 6
LLANDUDNO TO CONWY

DESCRIPTION A 8½ mile highly scenic linear walk following a delightful section of the Coast Path from Llandudno to the medieval walled town of Conwy, returning (or starting) by regular bus [14,15 & 19 – a more limited service on Sundays – visit: www.conwy.gov.uk/publictransport]. From the North Shore the route follows spectacular Marine Drive around the Great Orme (cafe midway) to West Shore. It then follows the shoreline Conwy Estuary Trail to Deganwy and along the estuary edge, before crossing the river into Conwy. Allow about 5 hours. The route can easily be broken down into three shorter walks linked to bus services or extended to Conwy Nature Reserve.
START Cenotaph, northern end of the North Shore Promenade, Llandudno [SH 782826].

The stunning medieval fortified walled town of Conwy standing near the mouth of the Afon Conwy estuary against a backdrop of mountains, is a designated World Heritage Site. Its impressive late 13thC castle

WALKS 5 & 6

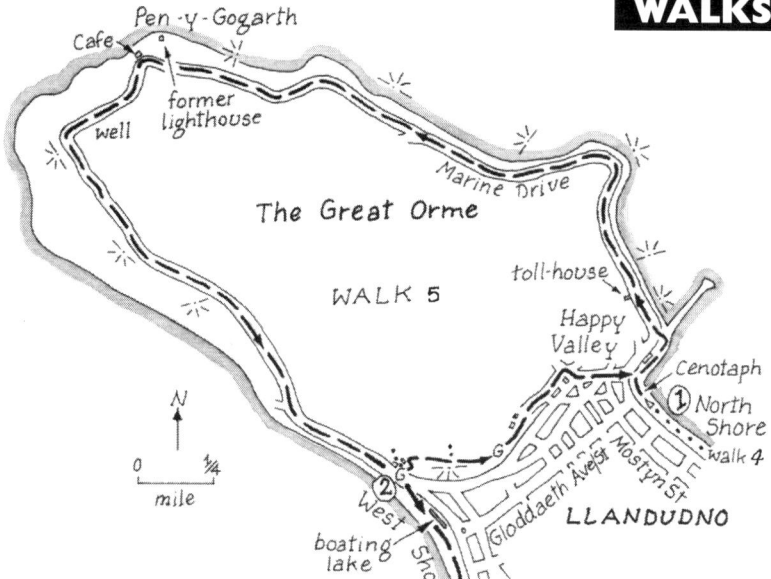

was built for Edward I to strengthen his conquest of Wales, and the walls, over ¾ mile in length, originally with 22 towers enclosed a new town occupied by English settlers. Crossing the estuary are two historic bridges built by renowned engineers: Thomas Telford's graceful suspension bridge (1826) and the adjacent tubular railway bridge built by Robert Stephenson (1849). Conwy was once an important port and boats still continue the town's mussel fishing tradition. Today the estuary and marina are home to many small pleasure boats and yachts.

1 Follow instructions in paragraph **1** of Walk 5.

2 Continue along the pavement, then go along the promenade at West Shore past the boating lake – *with two small peaks ahead marking the site of Deganwy Castle (See Walk 10).* After a car park, with a cafe nearby, continue along the wide shoreline Conwy Estuary Trail beneath dunes – *enjoying fine views across to Conwy mountain, along the coast to Penmaenmawr, and across to Anglesey.* Eventually you reach a shoreline road in Deganwy. *For centuries, until Telford's suspension bridge was opened in 1826, a ferry operated across the tidal river from here. A new river taxi service to Conwy began here in 2010.* At the railway crossing go past the rear of toilets and continue with the estuary trail – *with a good view across to Conwy Marina.* After passing Deganwy Quay with its hidden marina the trail continues above the edge of the estuary – *enjoying good views to Conwy and its impressive castle.* Eventually the walkway splits at an information board just beyond the Conwy tunnel monument. (The left fork extends the recreational route to Conwy Nature Reserve.) Bear RIGHT to follow the lower of two pathways through gardens, then up to cross the bridge over the river to enter Conwy.

WALK 7
CONWY

DESCRIPTION A 4½ mile walk of great variety exploring the medieval fortified walled town of Conwy, then extending to its modern Marina and the sand dunes of Conwy Morfa at the mouth of the estuary, returning via attractive woodland and the stunning town walls. Allow about 2½ hours. Shorter walk options.
START Conwy Visitor Centre [SH 781774] – located near the railway station.

Conwy, standing near the mouth of the Afon Conwy estuary, is a designated World Heritage Site. Its impressive late 13thC castle was built for Edward I to strengthen his conquest of Wales, and the walls, over ¾ mile in length, originally with 22 towers enclosed a new town occupied by English settlers. Conwy was once an important port and boats still continue the town's mussel fishing tradition.

Conwy Marina was created from a specially excavated casting basin, where tube sections of the Conwy tunnel (1991) were built before being floated into position in the river. Conwy Morfa, a protected area of sand dunes, has an interesting history. During the 19thC people worked here extracting pearls from mussels. In 1898 Royal Welsh Fusiliers had a camp here and evidence of their rifle range remains. In 1944 about 900 men worked on the Morfa in great secrecy building sections of the floating harbour, codenamed Mulberry, which was used in D-Day landings in Normandy.

1 Head towards a nearby tower then follow a cobbled path through an archway and continue beneath the town walls to reach an old crane at good viewpoint of the castle. Retrace your steps then climb up the tower and walk along the walls. After descending go along the car park edge to the castle entrance and Tourist Information Centre. Descend to the lower entrance and cross to the pavement opposite beneath the castle. Use the nearby Pelican crossing and go through the archway ahead, then continue over Pont Conwy to enjoy views along the estuary. *Nearby are Thomas Telford's graceful suspension bridge (1826) alongside Robert Stephenson's tubular railway bridge.* Retrace your steps then descend to the quayside. Go past Conwy Mussels, toilets, the Liverpool Arms and the Smallest House to pass under the walls. Go up the road then turn RIGHT on the signposted North Wales Path. Follow the delightful Marine Walk beneath Bodlondeb Wood – *created by Albert Wood who lived at nearby Bodlondeb Hall, built in 1877* – and along the edge of the estuary, with its many moored yachts – *enjoying good views back to the castle, then to the mouth of the estuary with the Great Orme beyond, and across to Deganwy Quay marina.* Later the walkway bends inland to an information board at the corner of Bodlonded Wood.

2 Continue along the walkway past the blue bridge to the entrance to Ysgol Aberconwy and follow the road RIGHT to go over the A55. At Marina Village turn RIGHT to reach The Mulberry (a good refreshment stop) and access to the marina. Continue round the edge of the marina to its far corner by the estuary, then turn LEFT. Go past the top of the slipway and jetty. Continue on a path along the edge of the dunes, soon alongside the perimeter fence of the golf course to reach the edge of Conwy Bay. The path now bends away from the estuary above the rocky shoreline – *with views to Conwy Mountain and the quarried coastal hills above Penmaenmawr.* At an old concrete rifle butt turn LEFT to join a nearby stony track. Follow it across the middle of the golf course, then an access road to the nearby road at Marina Village. Follow it to a roundabout and on to join your outward route. Follow it back to point 2.

and go up steps, then turn LEFT along Twr Llewelyn. At the junction turn RIGHT back to the start.

WALKS 7 & 8

WALK 8
CONWY MORFA

DESCRIPTION A delightful 2 mile walk along the beach at low tide to the marina, returning by a path through the dunes, offering great views. Allow about 1½ hours.

START Conwy Morfa car park [SH 762787] or Marina car park [SH 774790].

DIRECTIONS From junction 17 of the A55 follow signs for the Marina, then for Aberconwy Park to reach the beach car park and toilets.

From the entrance go along the signposted path to an access point onto the beach. Continue beneath the dunes, then rocky foreshore, bending towards the estuary and Deganwy opposite. Just before a jetty go to the top of a slipway, then continue above the beach to the corner of the marina. Return to the slipway then follow a path along the top of the dunes, soon alongside the perimeter fence of the golf course. After passing two old concrete rifle butts the path continues beside the dunes to the start.

3 Enter Bodlondeb Wood and follow the path ahead up the woodland edge, then turn LEFT up a stepped path. At a crossroad of paths by a seat, follow a path LEFT up to paths by post 14N. Turn LEFT and follow the wide path round the wooded slope, past post 16 Q then a seat at a good viewpoint, after which it bends south past a path on the left and rises. Soon take its left fork down the wood edge past post 18C to cross a road behind Bodlondeb Hall. Follow formal paths round the left side of the building, then the left edge of parkland to join the road. Follow it to the main road. Turn LEFT through the nearby archway, then go up steps onto the town walls. First descend to the end overlooking the river, then return to follow the western walls up to a corner tower, from where there is a dramatic descent After passing further towers the walls level out and you are forced to descend. Go through the wall gap ahead onto the railway station platform. Pass under the road bridge

Town walls

T*raeth Lafan*, lying between Llanfairfechan and Bangor, is a designated Site of Special Scientific Interest and a Special Protection area. It attracts huge flocks of birds, including many species of wildfowl and wading birds during spring and autumn migration, and large numbers of overwintering waders. The sand, shingle, saltmarsh and extensive mudflats exposed at low tide stretching over towards Anglesey, offer an abundance of food – ie. ragworms, snails, cockles, and mussels, as well as fish – that attract and sustain a wide variety of birds. These include redshank, oystercatcher, shellduck, teal, wigeon, mallard, the great-crested grebe, merganser, goldeneye, lapwing, and curlew.

I Walk west along the promenade and over the river where it joins the sea to a wooden shelter, displaying information on birds that you might see. Follow the concrete walkway by the sea wall past a small lake, then continue along the surfaced walkway above the rocky shore past woodland – enjoying views across to Puffin Island and Anglesey, along the coast to Penrhyn Castle and Bangor pier, and inland to the Carneddau mountains – to its end at a seat. Nearby is a shingle ridge and spit known locally as 'Shell Island', where oystercatchers and ringed plover roost. Access is restricted during March to July,

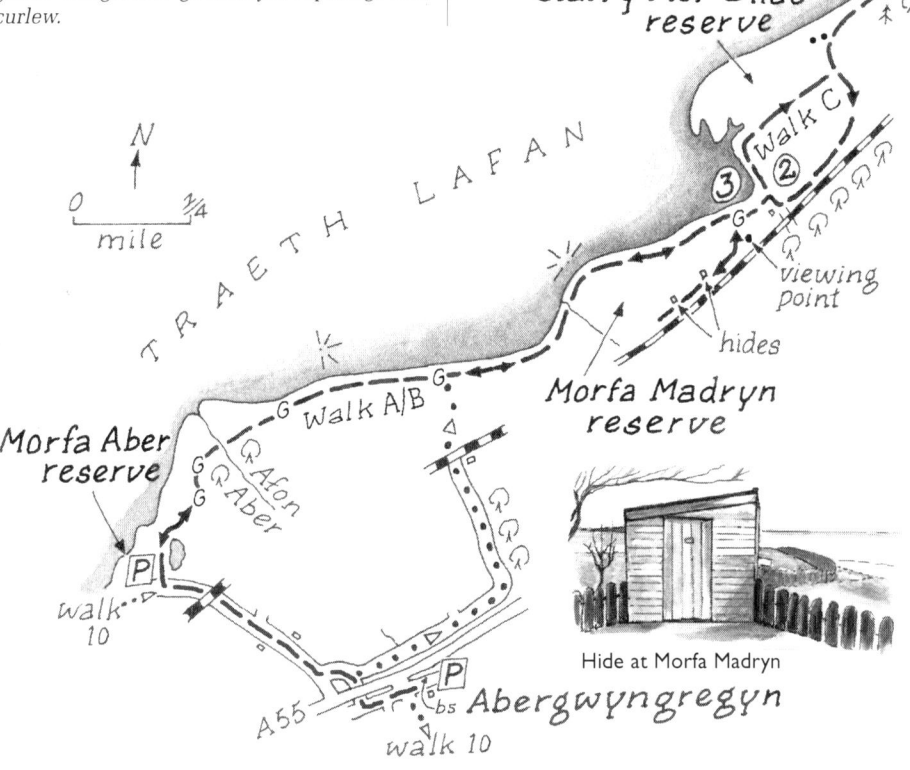

Hide at Morfa Madryn

There are four designated nature reserves linked by the Coastal Path – the Spinnies at Aber Ogwen, Morfa Aber, Morfa Madryn – all containing hides for discreet viewing of birds – and the open saltmarsh reserve of Glan y Mor Elias.

and at high tide August to February, to avoid disturbance to birds. Continue along the wide embanked green path, known as 'The Cob', bending away from the shore. Follow it along the edge of Glan y Mor Elias Saltmarsh Nature Reserve, then continue with the path close to the railway line.

WALK 9

TRAETH LAFAN NATURE RESERVES

DESCRIPTION A choice of 6 mile (**A**), 4½ mile (**B**) or 3 mile (**C**) walks featuring important coastal nature reserves linked by the Coast Path, lying alongside the unspoilt Traeth Lafan (Lavan Sands), internationally renowned for its birdlife. Walk A is a there and back route with variations that visits three nature reserves. Allow about 3 hours plus time for bird watching. Walk B is a linear walk that extends to Abergwyngregyn for catching the regular X5 bus back to Llanfairfechan. Walk C is a popular local stroll to the first two reserves. The Coast Path from Llanfairfechan to Glan y Mor Elias is surfaced then grassed, suitable for strong wheelchairs. Binoculars are recommended. Keep dogs under strict control and away from any birds. Where possible, time your walk to avoid high tide in order not to disturb birds roosting on the narrow upper shore.

START Promenade, Llanfairfechan [SH 679754].

DIRECTIONS At traffic lights in the centre of Llanfairfechan, turn down Station Road, go under the railway by the station, to reach a large car park with toilets and café by the promenade.

The Coast Path continues along a wide gated section, then by the shore, crosses a large footbridge over the Afon Aber by woodland, then continues to the entrance to Morfa Aber Reserve. For **Walk A** return along the Coast Path to the entrance to Morfa Madryn Reserve at point 3, then continue with Walk C through Glan y Mor Elias Reserve back to the start. For a variation follow roads as shown to cross the main railway line, taking heed of the warning signs, then path to rejoin the Coast Path. (For **Walk B** follow roads to pass under the A55 into Abergwyngregyn. Turn left past a slip road to a bus shelter. Catch the X5 to alight just before the traffic lights in Llanfairfechan. Return down Station Road.)

2 At the corner of the reserve, just beyond an information board, cross a stream and turn RIGHT to follow the slate fence round to the gated entrance to Morfa Madryn Nature Reserve – *consisting of landscaped shallow pools and low lying marshy fields*. From the information board follow a stony path alongside the reserve perimeter to a hide and on to reach the further of two hides for a viewing of the birds. *75 yards further along the path is an unusual stone memorial to two racehorses – Kingsford (1922-32) and Kinnaird (1920-31), the winner of 22 and 19 races respectively*. Retrace your steps, and after the path bends towards the shore, go up steps on your right to a viewing area looking over the reserve, then return to the reserve entrance.

3 For **Walk C** return to the Glan y Mor Elias information board, then turn LEFT along the grassy bank overlooking the mudflats. Just before an inlet, bear RIGHT along the grass embankment – *giving excellent views of birds feeding on the saltmarsh and in the deep channels which bisect it* – to join your outward path. Follow it back to the lake at Llanfairfechan, then go round its right hand side to the start – passing an interesting old plaque in the wall reflecting a different era of users of this walkway at the beginning of the 20th C.

For **Walks A/B** follow the shoreline Coast Path west towards Penrhyn Castle, initially beside the Reserve's perimeter fence, then past a section of stone wall to where you meet the alternative return path shown.

T*raeth Lafan (Lavan Sands) lying between Llanfairfechan and Bangor, is a designated Special Site of Scientific Interest and a Special Protection Area. It attracts huge flocks of birds, including many species of wildfowl and wading birds during spring and autumn migration, and large numbers of overwintering waders. The sand, shingle, saltmarsh and extensive mudflats exposed at low tide stretching over towards Anglesey, offer an abundance of food – i.e. ragworms, snails, cockles, and mussels, as well as fish – that attract and sustain a wide variety of birds. The Spinnies and Morfa Aber Nature Reserves contain hides for the discreet viewing of birds.*

1 Head east from the car park to follow the Coast Path along the shingle shoreline – with views across to Beaumaris and Puffin island. As you pass round beneath small cliffs, new views unfold along the coast to the Great Orme. The path then continues on grass past a small wood, and on alongside an attractive slate boundary. Follow the grassy foreshore to its end, then continue along the rocky shore. *In 1648, this area was the scene of a battle, known as Y Dalar Hir (the long front) which saw Parliamentarian troops defeat Royalist forces.* After crossing a stream, go up onto a grass embankment to soon join an access track by a house. *Prior to the building of Telford's suspension bridge over the Menai Straits in 1826, crossing to and from the mainland was hazardous. Mail and travellers to Anglesey and Ireland were ferried from near here to Beaumaris. Cattle would be driven across Traeth Lafan when the channel was at its narrowest, risking quicksand and the ravages of the fast incoming tide.* Follow the track to Morfa Aber reserve. Go along the road, passing under the railway. At a junction, continue up the road.

At the next junction, turn LEFT towards Abergwyngregyn to pass under the A55. Turn LEFT. (For the low level road alternative turn right.)

2 Shortly turn RIGHT, signposted to Aber Falls, then take the next road on the right through the village, past Yr Hen Felin Café & Information Centre, then just past Nant y Felin on the left take a signposted path through a small gate up on the right. Go up its left fork which rises steeply up the hillside to a small gate. *Here are extensive views over Traeth Lafan and along the coast from the Great Orme to Bangor.* Continue up the path to a waymarked path junction at a stony track, then follow it up the hillside.

WALK 10

WALK 10
TRAETH LAFAN

DESCRIPTION A 7½ mile walk of contrasting coastal and upland scenery, featuring a section of unspoilt coast, nature reserves, extensive birdlife, and foothills offering great views. The route follows the Coast Path east for 3 miles along the shoreline of Traeth Lafan to Morfa Aber nature reserve, before heading inland to Abergwyngregyn. After a short steep climb to about 800 feet it then follows the scenic high-level North Wales Path across the open slopes of the northern Carneddau foothills, before descending to Tan-y-Lon and following field paths to The Spinnies nature reserve. Allow about 4½ hours. A lower level alternative to the North Wales Path section is to follow quiet lanes from Aber. Binoculars are recommended. Where possible, time your walk to avoid high tide in order not to disturb birds roosting on the narrow upper shore, and keep dogs under strict control.
START Aber Ogwen car park [SH 616724] or Abergwyngregyn [SH 656728].
DIRECTIONS From Bangor, turn off the A5122 by Penrhyn Castle towards Tal-y-Bont, passing over the river. Ignore turnings into Tal-y-Bont, then take a road on the left, signposted 'Nature Reserve'. Go past the reserve to the shore car park. If you are starting from Abergwyngregyn there is a formal roadside car park beyond the bus stop, as shown.

3 At the top turn RIGHT and follow the level green track on the waymarked NWP through gates ahead, then across the hillside to a kissing gate. Continue by the fence across open upland pasture, crossing two ladder-stiles – *enjoying panoramic coastal views* – then follow the faint green track passing above a steep side valley. When the track bends right down towards the coast, cross the ladder-stile ahead. Follow the fence on your right up to gates by pylons. Keep on with the level green track, crossing two ladder-stiles. The track now makes a long gentle descent towards the coast, then bends west and continues across the open slopes to a forest corner, then descends to a lane by Bronydd Isaf. Turn LEFT down the lane, and at a junction, turn RIGHT and follow the road down the attractive wooded valley and on to reach Hendre – *built in 1860 for the Penrhyn estate for horse breeding and training*. Follow the road down and across the A55.

4 Just before a junction at Tan-y-Lon, take a signposted path over a stile on the right. Bear RIGHT and follow the concrete track round to its end. Continue ahead along a green track, through a wood, under a railway line and over a stile into a field. Go half-RIGHT to cross a ladder-stile, then turn LEFT to walk along the field edge. Go through a kissing gate at the end of a small wood, then go straight across the next field and through a gate in the boundary ahead. Follow the boundary on your right, continuing with a track – *with Penrhyn Castle, built between 1819-35 from wealth accrued from the slate industry, prominent on the skyline* – to pass farm buildings. Follow the waymarked path through a gate, passing to the left of the house to a road. Turn RIGHT to reach the entrance to The Spinnies nature reserve. Follow the path through the reserve to the hide to watch the birds on the lagoon, then go through shrubs to reach the Ogwen estuary. Follow the shoreline back to the start.

15

WALK 11
BWRDD ARTHUR

DESCRIPTION A 5 mile meandering and undulating walk to visit an Iron Age hillfort (538 feet/164 metres), now accessible as an Open Access area, offering panoramic views, returning on the Coastal Path. Allow about 3 hours.
START Traeth Coch (east) beach car park, Anglesey. [SH 568806].
DIRECTIONS The car park with toilets and seasonal café is reached by a steep minor road from the northern end of Llanddona.

*B*wrdd Arthur *(Arthur's Table) is a small limestone hill containing the remains of an Iron Age hillfort and hut circles.*

1 Return along the road, soon bending inland. Later take a signposted path along a track past a cottage to a kissing gate at its end. Follow the field path through further kissing gates to reach a track by a house. Turn RIGHT up a hedge/tree-lined path to a house. Go past its right-hand side and up to a kissing gate by an old ruin. Just beyond go up the path's left fork to a waymarked junction. Turn LEFT up the path to a kissing gate, then go up the road. At the T-junction turn LEFT down the road. On the bend take the signposted bridleway through the entrance to Ysgubor Penrallt, then go down the track's left fork. Shortly the tree-lined bridleway narrows. At an old gate it does a U-turn and heads north to eventually emerge at the entrance to Hafod Wen. Go down its access track.

2 Just before Tros yr Afon turn RIGHT up steps and follow the path up to join an access track which rises to a road. Go up the road and past a transmitter mast. At the junction turn LEFT then cross a stile beneath Bwrdd Arthur. Follow a side path beside the fence up onto the hillfort for panoramic views from its trig point and eastern ramparts, then return to the stile. Now follow the path along Bwrdd Arthur's lower western slopes. At a waymarker post turn sharp LEFT down a farm track, now on the Coast Path, to a ladder-stile. Follow the path along the field edge to a ladder-stile, then down to a kissing gate to enter Bryn Offa (NT) grazed by ponies. The path descends the gorse-covered hillside to join a farm track.

3 Follow it LEFT, initially descending, to reach a house at a signposted path junction. Turn RIGHT and follow the Coast Path down a track. When it bends right keep ahead to go through a gate just before a cottage. Bear RIGHT to follow the path to a ladder-stile and on down the field to a kissing gate. Go along the low cliffs to a kissing gate, then the edge of the rocky shore to cross a footbridge over a stream to reach a road. Follow it RIGHT back to the start.

WALKS 11 & 12

WALK 12
YNYS LLANDDWYN

DESCRIPTION A 4½ mile (**A**) or 3¾ mile (**B**) walk featuring attractive forest, an award winning beach, panoramic views and a visit to the historic romantic Llanddwyn island, accessible except at high tide. Allow about 3 hours.
START Newborough Forest car park, Anglesey [SH 406635].
DIRECTIONS From the centre of Newborough follow a minor road signposted to the beach, later through the forest, to a large car park.

vated in 1975. Nearby are cottages (now containing an exhibition) built in the mid-19thC for pilots who guided ships through the Menai Strait. Outside is a cannon used to call the crew of a lifeboat based here from 1840 until 1903. More recently in 2004 the island was used as a film location for the romantic thriller 'Half Light', starring Demi Moore.

1 From an information board near the car park entrance follow the road then track through the forest to an informal beach car park. Follow the beach round to a covered information board on Llanddwyn Island. Just beyond turn LEFT and follow the waymarked Ynys Llanddwyn path clockwise round the island. Afterwards return along the beach

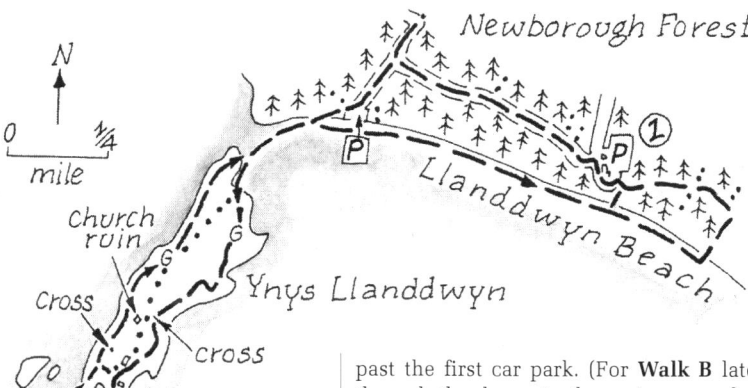

past the first car park. (For **Walk B** later go through the dunes to the main car park.) For **Walk A** continue east along the beach then at the forest corner follow the waymarked Coast Path up through the dunes. Shortly, follow the Coast Path LEFT through the trees and along a track back to the start.

L<i>landdwyn is named after St Dwynwen, patron saint of Welsh lovers, who allegedly lived here in the 5thC, and whose legend attracted pilgrims here in later centuries. Today this small beautiful island is a fascinating place to visit, with superb views. It contains the ruins of a 16thC church dedicated to St Dwynwen and two large crosses. At its tip are an early 19thC stone beacon tower, now with a modern light, and a windmill shaped lighthouse built in 1845, which was deacti-</i>

Pilots' cottages

WALK 13
TRAETH LLYDAN & ST GWENFAEN'S WELL

DESCRIPTION A 5½ mile walk (**A**) featuring the Anglesey Coast Path, beaches, an ancient well, and a country pub en route. Allow about 3½ hours. The route can easily be undertaken as two shorter walks of 3½ miles (**B**) and 2½ miles (**C**) using the link road between Borthwen and Rhoscolyn.
START Car park Borthwen, Anglesey [SH 272752].
DIRECTIONS From the B4545 at Four Mile Bridge take the minor road to Rhoscolyn. Go past The White Eagle and follow the road to the beach car park at its end.

1 Return along the road, then take the signposted enclosed Coast Path on the right. (For **Walk C** follow the road to Rhoscolyn.) At a waymarked path junction go through a blue gate ahead and follow the path to houses. Go along a track, then at a junction, follow the track RIGHT between bungalows to a kissing gate. Follow the main path across the headland, then along the low cliffs round to Porth Cae-du. Here take the right fork to a kissing gate. After crossing sleeper bridges go up through gorse and on to another kissing gate. Continue with the Coast Path – *with views across to Rhosneigr and RAF Valley* – to eventually pass a flagpole. Take the signposted path onto Traeth Llydan and walk along the edge of the beach.

2 After 200 yards, take a stepped path up the dunes and go through the pine forest, leaving it by a kissing gate. After another kissing gate the path heads to the ruined farm of Bryn-y-bar. Continue along its access track. It later becomes a lane, passes a wood, then the permissive Coast Path. At a road take its right fork. After the road kinks go through a kissing gate on the left by an access track. Follow the path to a kissing gate, then to a drive and on to another kissing gate. Go across the field to a kissing gate, then angle LEFT to a kissing gate by a cottage at Rhoscolyn. (For **Walk B** follow the road ahead.) Follow the road RIGHT past The White Eagle pub. At the next junction turn LEFT to St Gwenfaen's church.

3 Follow the minor road round the church to its end, then continue along the track. Just before Tywrideen go through a kissing gate on the right then descend to another. Turn LEFT and follow the waymarked path round Tywrideen's boundary. At the corner by the house, turn RIGHT along a walled green track to a kissing gate. Follow the track down to its end then the waymarked path to a kissing gate onto the Coast Path.

4 Cross a nearby footbridge and go through a kissing gate. Follow the large stone wall across Rhoscolyn Head and round above Porth Gwalch to a kissing gate into a Open Access area. Follow the path to nearby St Gwenfaen's Well – *date unknown. It was said that throwing white quartz pebbles into the water cured mental disorders.* Either follow the main

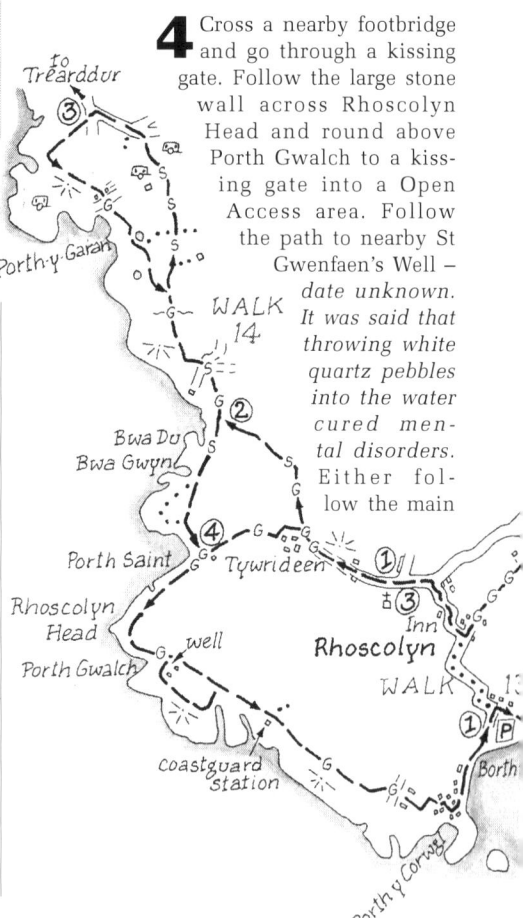

path or the top of the cliffs round to rejoin it, then continue to Rhoscolyn Coastguard Station. Keep ahead on the waymarked path, shortly descending to a kissing gate – *with a view across to Rhoscolyn Beacon on a tiny island*. Keep ahead, then 100 yards after the wall corner, angle LEFT to a kissing gate in the boundary corner. Follow the waymarked enclosed path to a lane by Bryn-Eithin's entrance and on to Boatmen's Cottage above Porth y Corwgl. Continue along the track down to the shore and along the edge of Borthwen Bay. After passing the last white cottage a raised path above the beach returns you to the road by the start.

WALK 14

BWA GWYN

DESCRIPTION A 3½ mile (**A**) or 1½ mile (**B**) walk exploring a coastal strip featuring the Coast Path, some of the oldest pre-Cambrian rocks in Britain, and two splendid sea arches – Bwa Du and Bwa Gwyn. Allow about 2 hours.
START St Gwenfaen's church, Rhoscolyn, Anglesey. [SH 268757].
DIRECTIONS From the B4545 take a choice of minor roads to Rhoscolyn, where there is parking near the church.

A church has stood on this site since *630AD when St Gwenfaen established her cell here. The present church dates from the 1870s using stones from an earlier 15thC church.*

1 Follow the minor road past the church to its end, then continue along the track. Just before Tywrideen go through a kissing gate on the right then descend to another. Go down the middle of the long field to another kissing gate. Keep ahead. At a waymarker post angle to cross a stile in the fence. Follow a path briefly by the fence, then on through bracken heading towards a large shoreline house, to descend between rocky ridges to join the Coast Path. (For **Walk B** follow it left to point **4**.)

2 Follow it RIGHT to a kissing gate, then on to a stile by the large house's gated driveway. Just beyond turn LEFT beside the wall, then at a waymarker post bear RIGHT, soon descending and continuing to a kissing gate. Keep ahead past a small sandy cove, then bear LEFT past the fence corner. At a waymarker post, leave the Coast Path by going half-RIGHT to pass through a gateway. Bear RIGHT with the path past a waymarker post. Take its waymarked left fork, over a cross-path and up a small gully to a stone stile. Follow the path to a stile just before a caravan site. The path continues past the caravan site's perimeter, past another on the right, to a caravan site's access road. Follow it LEFT to a road junction. Here, turn sharp LEFT at the entrance to Lee Caravan Park on the signposted path.

3 At a waymarker post turn RIGHT and follow the Coast Path to reach low cliffs. The path then passes above a caravan site. Just before Porth-y-garan ahead bear LEFT to a waymarker post then descend between static caravans to a lane and through a kissing gate opposite. Follow the Coast Path past a small reedy pool then a gate/path and on alongside the boundary. The path bends left at its corner, then right at a fence corner to join your outward route. Follow it back to point **2** – *later with a view of Bwa Gwyn ahead*. Now follow the Coast Path to a stile near the first arch of Bwa Du, past Bwa Gwyn then above Porth Saint.

4 Go through a kissing gate on the left and follow the waymarked path inland, soon along an old walled track up to a kissing gate and on towards Tywrideen. Just before the house, turn LEFT and follow the waymarked path round its boundary wall to join your outward route.

WALK 15
NORTH & SOUTH STACKS

DESCRIPTION An exhilarating 5 mile walk around rocky Holyhead Mountain, with its high cliffs and extensive views. The route follows the undulating Coast Path along the cliffs to the former Fog Signal Station at North Stack, then offers an optional climb to the mountain's summit (721 feet/220 metres), before continuing with the Coast Path to the headland overlooking South Stack lighthouse. It returns by other waymarked paths. Allow about 3½ hours. The paths are good, but this is real mountain terrain and best avoided in poor visibility.

START Holyhead Breakwater Country Park Visitor Centre [SH 226833].

DIRECTIONS The Country Park lies beneath Holyhead Mountain and is signposted from the northern end of Holyhead.

In the 19th century steps were taken to establish navigational aids on Holyhead Mountain to help protect the coastal shipping and assist ships travelling between Ireland and Holyhead. In 1809 Trinity House, at a cost of £12,000, established a lighthouse on South Stack, a small rocky island connected to the mainland by a small bridge. In 1938 its oil lamps were replaced by electric powered lamps, then in 1987 its light became fully automated. The 19thC Fog Signal Station built on the cliffs at North Stack is now a private residence.

1 Go through a wall gap at the end of the first car park, then follow a path past Llyn Llwynog to a kissing gate. Turn LEFT along a track to be joined by the Coast Path, then go through a kissing gate and continue on the Coast Path. Later it crosses the steep slopes above the sea, then rises past a small stone building, increasingly more steeply, to a cross-path. Follow it RIGHT, soon rising, then take the right fork down to the former North Stack fog signal station (or continue on the upper fork). Follow a rough stony track zig-zagging up the mountainside, later levelling out. At a crossroad of tracks/paths, turn RIGHT, then take the left fork up the rocky slopes, then through gorse and heather to a good viewpoint towards South Stack. The Coast Path then descends – *with the trig point on the summit visible ahead* – and crosses an area of heather. Go up the right fork.

2 On a small rise is a waymarker post signing a short steep climb to the summit, returning via another path signed to South Stack, passing the ramparts of the Iron Age hillfort. The Coast Path now descends past side paths to reach a waymarked path junction below a building and transmitter mast. Follow the Coast Path to cross a road and on past small masts, soon descending. It continues across the headland past three reedy pools to reach a lookout shelter overlooking South Stack lighthouse. Follow a path down to the road. *Here there is an optional descent via 400 steps to South Stack.* Go along the road then take a signposted path up a road on the left, later continuing along a stony track near the road to a familiar crossroad of paths. Here turn RIGHT and follow the waymarked 'Circular Walk' path past side paths, later bending right beneath Holyhead Mountain, then rising across its shoulder, past side paths and continuing near a wall on your left.

3 At the wall corner by a waymarker post keep ahead. Later at path crossroads continue ahead with the walled path, soon descending past a water tank to a lane/track junction. Go down the lane. At the junction, turn LEFT. At the lane end by Gornish bear LEFT on an enclosed path. Very soon, at a junction, turn RIGHT, then LEFT at the next. Descend between gorse, then via steps. Bear LEFT by a large stone to the nearby road. Cross it, go past the small reservoir, then go along the side of Llyn Llwynog.

WALKS 15 & 16

1 Go through a wall gap at the end of the first car park, then follow a path past Llyn Llwynog to a kissing gate. Turn LEFT along a track past the Coast Path then a memorial to a 1944 aeroplane crash. After a kissing gate the narrow stony track rises steadily before levelling out. For **Walk A** continue down to a waymarked track/path junction, then follow the Coast Path up to point 2. For **Walks B/C**, after passing telegraph pole 816813 as the track starts to level out, go up a path on the left to head back towards Holyhead. At a major path crossroads, turn RIGHT and follow the path up the slope, soon levelling out. **Walk B** takes the right fork to join the Coast Path to point **2**. (For **Walk C** take the left fork, then follow a cross path LEFT, initially steeply, to the summit. With the trig point to your left and the old Roman wall to your right, go straight ahead past a stone shelter to follow a clear path on a steep descent down the mountain's rocky south eastern slope to another path. Soon in a flattish area take the left fork down towards two distant reservoirs. After a short steep descent a more level path takes you to a wall gap. Beyond at a crossroad of paths, turn LEFT and follow instructions in paragraph **3** of **Walk 15**.)

WALK 16
HOLYHEAD MOUNTAIN

DESCRIPTION A choice of 2¾ (**A**), 2¼ (**B**) or 2½ (**C**) meandering walks to the summit of Holyhead Mountain (721 feet/220 metres), with its remains of a Roman watchtower and Iron Age hillfort, and great views. **Walks A & B** take the signed ascent/descent from the Coast Path. **Walk C** has a more demanding rocky descent. Allow about 2 hours. Despite its low height this is real mountain terrain and should be avoided in poor visibility.
START As **Walk 15**.

2 At the top of the rise, take the signed short steep climb to the summit, returning via another path signed to South Stack, passing the ramparts of an Iron Age hillfort Follow the Coast Path LEFT, then at a waymarker post, turn LEFT and follow a path beneath the mountain's rocky western slopes, popular with rock climbers, soon descending to a path junction. Turn LEFT along the waymarked path, soon rising across the mountain's shoulder and continuing near a wall on your left. Now follow instructions in paragraph **3** of **Walk 15**.

WALK 17
CARMEL HEAD

DESCRIPTION A 5 mile walk (**A**) across country to Hen Borth then following the Coast Path to and around Carmel Head, part of the Mynachdy estate owned by the National Trust. It visits the 'White Ladies' pilot beacons and 19thC copper mine chimney, and reaches a high viewpoint above Porth yr Hwch. The more rugged undulating next section of the Coast Path to Llyn y Fydlyn is only open 1 Feb–14 Sept. Allow about 3½ hours. An alternative attractive 3½ mile walk (**B**) is included. The main route can easily be extended to Trwyn Cemlyn (an additional 2½ miles).

START National Trust Mynachdy car park, Anglesey. SH 303914].

DIRECTIONS Turn off the A5025 to Llanfairynghornwy. Go through the village, past a turn on the left, then a no through road on the right to find the NT car park on the right at a bend. It can also be accessed from the south.

The sea off Carmel Head, the remote north-western tip of Anglesey, with its submerged rocks, treacherous currents, and small islands, is among the most dangerous in Britain, resulting in many shipwrecks. In 1716, as an aid to navigation, a private entrepreneur built a coal beacon on The Skerries, a long island lying in the shipping lane between Liverpool and Ireland It was replaced by a new lighthouse with oil lamps and reflectors in 1804. It was the last privately owned lighthouse in Britain when it was sold Trinity House in 1841. The light was automated in 1987. In the 1860s, two large white triangular stone pillars, known as the 'White Ladies ' were erected on the headland. When aligned with a third marker on West Mouse island they provided an exact bearing of Coal Rock, a hazard to shipping.

1 Turn LEFT along the road. At a junction go along the no through road, past a house and on to enter the farmyard at Mynachdy. (For **Walk B** turn left and follow the track up to a ladder-stile, then to a stile/gate and on across open ground. Follow it round the dam of a reedy reservoir up to a ladder-stile. Angle left to a stile/gate, then keep ahead to follow a faint level green track to a stile/gate near a ruin. Continue ahead to pass under the higher of the 'White Ladies' to join the Coast path at the old mine chimney. Follow instructions from the third sentence in paragraph 2 up to point **3**.) For **Walk A** turn RIGHT to go through a gate by outbuildings. Follow the farm track through fields to Hen Felin, then its access track to the road. Go through a kissing gate on the left. Follow the path to join the Coast path at Hen Borth.

2 Follow the Coast path west through kissing gates to enter Mynachdy estate and eventually reach Carmel Head and the 'White Ladies'. After passing the lower pillar follow the waymarked path to a footbridge and across to the former copper mine chimney. Follow the waymarked Coast path up to pass an old gatepost and a ruin, then across the headland. Later you head south – *with a view of Holyhead Mountain* – and climb up to a prominent summit offering extensive views down the coast to Holyhead.

3 Head south-east down to a kissing gate above Porthyr Hwch. The Coast path descends to another kissing gate, then rises along a heather rocky ridge, before descending and heading seawards, passing a tall concrete post. It then turns inland towards Llyn y Fydlyn and bends down to a kissing gate. Nearby is Ynys y Fydlyn sea arch. At the next corner turn LEFT up a rough track, soon taking its left fork up by the forest. When it fades keep ahead to pass the forest corner, soon joining a path which then bends right to a fence corner. Follow the fence past an area of cleared forest to reach the car park.

WALKS 17 & 18

WALK 18
TRWYN CEMLYN & CARMEL HEAD

DESCRIPTION A 7 mile (**A**) or 6 mile (**B**) walk from Cemlyn Nature Reserve via Trwyn Cemlyn following the Coast Path to the 'White Ladies' (see Walk 17) on Carmel Head. **Walk A** continues up to a good viewpoint, then the summit of Penbrynyreglwys, before joining **Walk B** for the return via Mynachdy and an ancient church. Allow about 4 hours. Also included is an easy 2¼ mile walk to the church (**C**).
START Cemlyn car park (west). [SH 329935].
DIRECTIONS Cemlyn is signposted from the A5025 at the Douglas Inn, Tregele. Take the second road on the right. At the lagoon take the next no through road right to a large car park at its end. It is liable to flooding at high tide, so check times in advance.

Cemlyn Nature Reserve, owned by the National Trust, comprises a freshwater lagoon separated from the sea by a shingle ridge, except at high tide. It is one of the most important breeding sites for terns in Wales and attracts wildfowl in winter. The lagoon was previously managed as a wildfowl refuge by Capt. Vivian Hewitt, a pioneer aviator and dedicated ornithologist, who lived at nearby Bryn Aber. You can walk along the lagoon outside the tern breeding season (April–July inclusive) and on the seaward side of the ridge during that breeding period.

1 Take the signposted Coast Path along the track to Cemlyn Bay, then past a lifeboat commemorative monument. Follow a permissive path to the tip of Trwyn Cemlyn, returning south west above the shore – *enjoying good views to Carmel Head and The Skerries lighthouse.* Follow the Coast Path through kissing gates to eventually bend down to pass above Hen Borth. (For **Walk C** angle back across the field to visit the small church of St Rhwydrus. *The present church dates from the 12thC but was founded in the 6thC and dedicated to a little known saint from Ireland.* Afterwards head to the farm and go through the farmyard. Follow its access lane past the lagoon to a junction. Turn LEFT past Bryn Aber to the start.) For Walks **A/B** descend to Hen Borth's pebbly beach.

2 Follow instructions in paragraph **2** of **Walk 17** to point **3**. (For **Walk B**, when you reach the former 19thC copper mine chimney turn sharp left along a green track, passing beneath the other pillar to reach a stile/gate. Follow the faint track to another stile/gate. Angle right to a ladder-stile, then follow the track past the remains of a reedy reservoir and on to Mynachdy farm. Follow a farm track eastwards through fields to Hen Felin, then its access track to the road. Go through a kissing gate on the left. Follow the path to join your outward route at Hen Borth. Shortly head over to the church and follow **Walk C** back.)

3 For **Walk A** head east and work your way up the small cairn on the top of Penbrynyreglwys. Go north a little further then head north east down towards the chimney to join **Walk B** for the return – see above.)

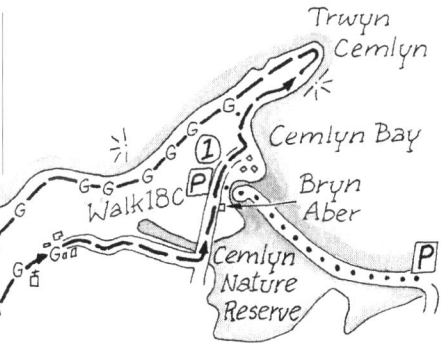

WALK 19
PORTH LLANLLEIANA & LLANBADRIG CHURCH

DESCRIPTION A 3½ mile walk through attractive countryside past The Vineyard, offering Welsh wine tasting and refreshments (telephone 01407 710416 for opening times) to former porcelain works at Porth Llanlleaina. It then returns along the stunning cliff-top Anglesey Coast Path via old Llanbadrig Church. Allow about 2½ hours. A shorter 1½ mile walk is to follow the road up to the church and return along the Coastal Path.
START Cemaes Bay beach car park, Anglesey [SH 376937 or SH 373935].
DIRECTIONS The car park (also Llanbadrig Church/The Vineyard) is signposted off the A5025 along a single track road just east of Cemaes. For the alternative beach car park nearer Cemaes turn right at the bottom of the High Street, cross the river to find the park signposted.

1 Go back up the road to the junction and turn LEFT. (Alternatively, turn right and follow the field path described in paragraph 1 of **Walk 20**.) Go up the hill past the turning for the church – *enjoying good views* – to reach the Vineyard, then continue along the road to point **2**. Later, as the road bends right look for a hidden kissing gate on the left. Go up the field edge following the telegraph lines. Cross an access track and go through a gateway ahead. Now follow an old green track towards Dinas Gynfor then across a causeway over a reedy marsh. At a waymarked path junction, turn LEFT to reach the former Llanlleiana porcelain works, *which closed in 1920*. Now follow instructions in paragraph **6** of **Walk 20**.

WALK 20
PORTH WEN & DINAS GYNFOR

DESCRIPTION An exhilarating 6 mile (**A**) or 5½ mile (**B**) walk featuring one of Anglesey's best sections of rugged high cliffs. The outward route passes through attractive countryside then offers a choice of paths to Porth Wen, with Walk A offering the better views of the impressive old shoreline brickworks. In the early 20thC clay from nearby cliffs was used in three beehive kilns to make silica bricks for the steel industry and shipped from the small quay. It closed in 1924. The undulating cliff-top Coast Path is then followed west via the headland of Torllwyn and Hell's Mouth, to Dinas Gynfor with its Iron Age Hillfort. From the former Llanlleiana porcelain works, the Coastal Path continues past dramatic vertical cliffs and old Llanbadrig Church. Allow about 4 hours.
START As Walk 19.

WALKS 19 & 20

1 Go back up the road to the junction. Turn RIGHT then cross a stile on the left. Follow the path to another stile and onwards, soon crossing a small field to a kissing gate in the corner. Follow the boundary on your right to stiles. Cross the lawn of a nearby house, then its access track to a stile. Follow the path ahead through three fields to the road.

2 Turn RIGHT along the road, later rising steadily to a chapel at its highest point. Eventually you reach two signposted paths on the left. For **Walk B** take the first one through a kissing gate. Follow the enclosed path, soon bending down towards Porth Wen. After a kissing gate keep ahead to reach a waymarker post at a crossroad of paths overlooking the chimneys of the old brickworks at point **4**.

3 For **Walk A** go through the second kissing gate and up the field to another. Now angle RIGHT down the field to a further kissing gate – *with the first view of the old brickworks and sea arch*. Go down the slope ahead to a waymarker post and on to a metal kissing gate hidden in the boundary corner beyond. Continue down the slope to a crosspath below. Follow it RIGHT. Soon at a spring bear LEFT to a waymarker post, where you join the Coast Path. Follow the path down towards the brickworks to cross two sleeper bridges, then climb steadily to a kissing gate. Continue to another kissing gate and on to a waymarker post at a crossroad of paths.

4 Follow the Coast Path rising steadily towards a mast on Torllwyn headland. Take the right fork up past the mast to a great viewpoint – *along the coast and to Snowdonia, with a new view of the brickworks*. Return to the Coast Path. Follow it past an old winding house, then along the heather/bracken covered undercliff and a section of near vertical cliffs. After a good viewpoint to the tower on Dinas Gynfor the path then begins a long steady descent to Hell's Mouth. Go up the stepped path.

5 At the waymarked path junction you have a choice: **Route (a)**: turn RIGHT – *with a good view back along vertical cliffs* – and climb steadily to the top of Dinas Gynfor and on to the small tower – *offering views along the coast to Carmel Head and the lighthouse on the Skerries*. Soon the path descends steeply to the former Llanlleiana porcelain works. **Route (b)**: keep ahead with the delightful green path, soon angling down the bracken hillside. At a path junction bear RIGHT to reach the ruined porcelain works – which used china clay from Dinas Gynfor and closed in 1920.

6 Follow the Coast Path up steps and through a small gate. The path now rises in stages along the cliffs. After an undulating section of cliff-top path, you go through two kissing gates at a good viewpoint. Continue with the undulating path. After another kissing gate the path continues along the top of impressive vertical cliffs to pass round the wall of Llanbedrig church's graveyard. *Llanbadrig, founded in 440AD, is the only church in Wales dedicated to St Patrick of Ireland, allegedly after he sheltered in a cave here following being shipwrecked. The current church dates from the 12thC with later renovations and additions*. After visiting the church go down the road and through a kissing gate to follow the cliff-top Coast Path to the start.

WALK 21
MYNYDD EILIAN

DESCRIPTION A 7 mile (**A**) or 6½ mile (**B**) walk featuring one of Anglesey's high points, Mynydd Eilian (177 metres), offering panoramic views, a splendid section of the Coast Path, and Point Lynas lighthouse. Allow about 4½ hours. The permissive path to Porth yr Aber is closed for certain days (*Oct–Dec*) Enquiries: 01248 752300 or angleseycoastalpath.co.uk.
START Llaneilian car park, Anglesey [SH 474929].
DIRECTIONS The car park is on the right just before the road descends to the bay.

1 Go down the road past toilets to a mini-roundabout at Porth Eilian. Turn RIGHT past a good view along the bay to Point Lynas lighthouse, then take a signposted path (Eilian) on the right. Follow the path through fields, later rising to a lane. Turn RIGHT, then LEFT on the signposted enclosed path. It rises steadily, passes the entrance to Coed Avens then continues up an access track to reach a signposted crossroad of paths by an old barn.

2 Take the path up steps on the right (Copper Coast Trail) to a small gate. Go across the hillside to a small gate and another by an old building. Go up the track between houses, then continue along the minor road. Shortly go through a kissing gate up on the left. Go up the path, soon bending and rising steadily before continuing alongside the wall to a kissing gate. Cross the nearby ladder-stile, then follow the path up to a trig point on the top of Mynydd Eilian. Retrace your steps then continue down the path to a stone stile onto a minor road. Follow it LEFT. It later bends more SE and passes an access lane on the right. On a bend take a signposted path through a gate on the left. Angle RIGHT across two fields to reach another road. Follow it LEFT. At the junction, turn RIGHT towards Llysdulas. (Shortly for **Walk B** take the signposted path along the driveway to Rhos-mynach-isaf, from where the path descends an old green track to join the Coast Path at point **4**.)

3 At Gai Newyd by a junction you join the Coast Path /Copper Coastal Trail. Cross the ladder-stile and continue beside the wall to a ladder-stile/gate, then to another ladder-stile in a facing wall. Go slightly RIGHT to a telegraph pole, then follow the fence on your left down to a ladder-stile in the corner. Follow the stiled path along the edge of three fields to reach Porth yr Aber, with the tower on Ynys Dulas ahead – *built in 1824 as a refuge for shipwrecked sailors, stocked with food and water*. Turn LEFT and follow the fence round to a footbridge and kissing gate. Walk up the edge of the large field to cross a stile in the corner.

4 Continue with the waymarked Coast Path, later descending to a stile. The path crosses a large open area then climbs to a gateway at a waymarked cross-path. Continue with the Coast Path – *soon with Point Lynas lighthouse visible ahead*. Later, after crossing an old boundary you reach a good viewpoint overlooking Freshwater Bay. Here ignore a path heading up the slope, but keep ahead a few yards, then follow the path bending LEFT down through bracken into a side valley to a stile/footbridge. Follow the path to another stile. After a ladder-stile and a step stile the path continues to a kissing gate, where you are joined by Walk 22.

5 Walk ahead across the field. After the kissing gate, turn RIGHT and follow the path to Porth y Corwgl, then along the low cliffs, all too soon bending away to reach a kissing gate. Follow the path to a road. For the lighthouse turn RIGHT. Shortly go through a small gate on the left and follow a waymarked permissive path to the front of the lighthouse and nearby fog station. Return the same way or down the road. Follow the road back to the start.

WALK 21 & 22

WALK 22
POINT LYNAS

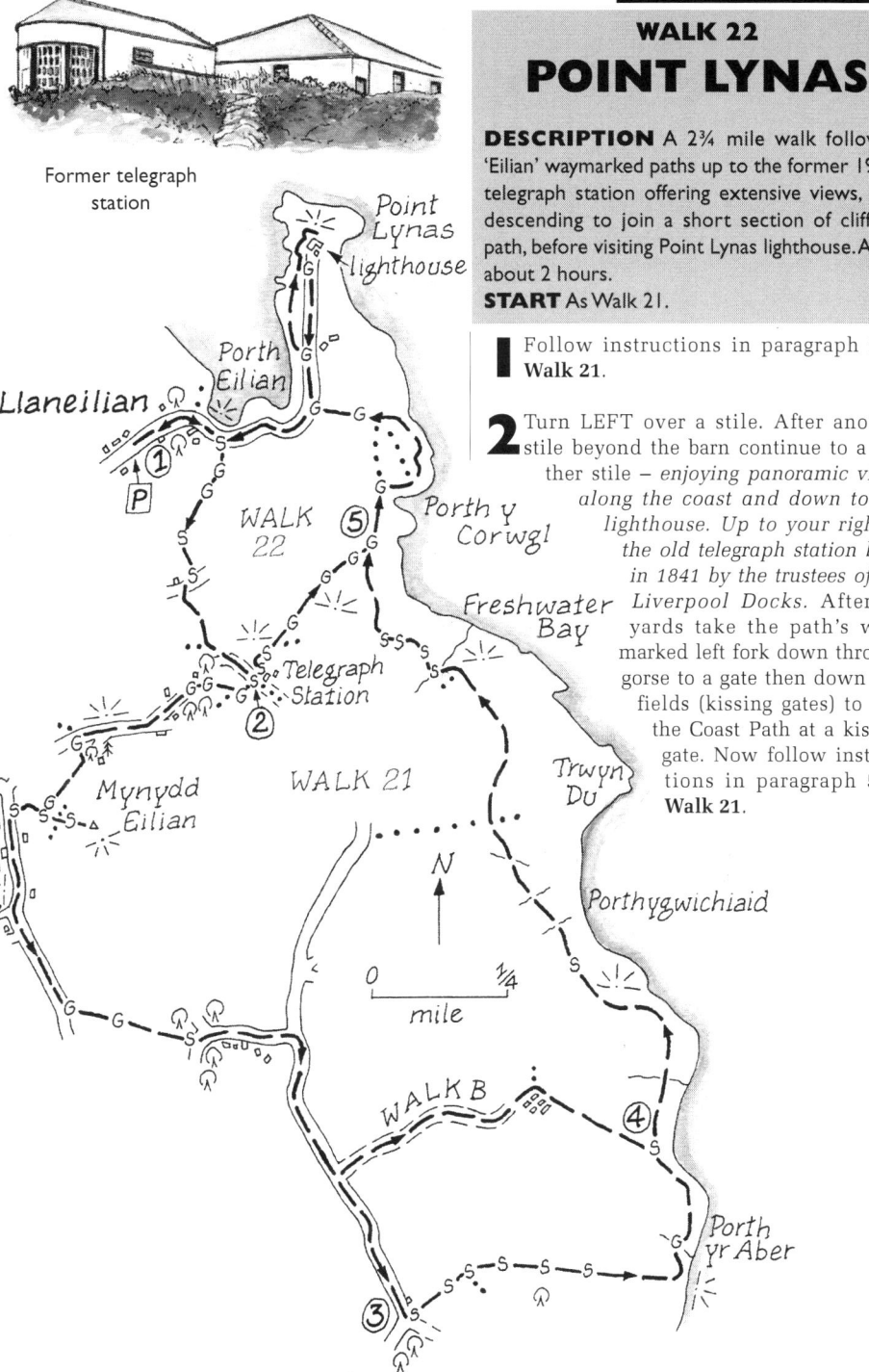

Former telegraph station

DESCRIPTION A 2¾ mile walk following 'Eilian' waymarked paths up to the former 19thC telegraph station offering extensive views, then descending to join a short section of cliff-top path, before visiting Point Lynas lighthouse. Allow about 2 hours.
START As Walk 21.

1 Follow instructions in paragraph **1** of **Walk 21**.

2 Turn LEFT over a stile. After another stile beyond the barn continue to a further stile – *enjoying panoramic views along the coast and down to the lighthouse. Up to your right is the old telegraph station built in 1841 by the trustees of the Liverpool Docks*. After 40 yards take the path's waymarked left fork down through gorse to a gate then down two fields (kissing gates) to join the Coast Path at a kissing gate. Now follow instructions in paragraph **5** of **Walk 21**.

WALK 23
TRAETH LLIGWY & DIN LLIGWY

DESCRIPTION A contrasting 4¼ mile walk full of interest, including two impressive ancient monuments. The route first follows the cliff top Coast Path past the Seawatch Centre and a memorial to the sinking of the Royal Charter in Porth Helaeth in 1859 to Traeth Lligwy car park, with toilets and seasonal café. It then returns via Din Lligwy and a Neolithic burial chamber. At Din Lligwy are the substantial remains of a Romano British settlement of stone buildings. This defended settlement containing round and rectangular huts of various dates, and a workshop, was mainly occupied during 4thC AD. Allow about 2½ hours.

START Moelfre car park, Anglesey [SH 512862].

DIRECTIONS On entering Moelfre on the A5108, turn left to find a choice of car parks. Use the one on the left by toilets.

*M*oelfre, once associated with a thriving herring industry, is perhaps best known for the sterling work of its lifeboat and crews. Since 1830 until the present day they have saved hundreds of shipwrecked mariners. Sadly it could not prevent the loss of over 400 lives and £300,000 of gold when the Royal Charter clipper on route from Melbourne to Liverpool was hit by a hurricane. It was seen as a national disaster attracting many visitors, including Charles Dickens.

1 Take the path leading from the toilets to the road. Cross to the left of the bus shelter opposite to take a pathway between houses to join the road by Ann's Pantry. Turn LEFT down the road, then go across the beach car park and follow a path down to rejoin the road. Follow it past the small pebbly beach up to the bend. Here take the signposted Coast Path round past houses then the original lifeboat station and Seawatch Centre – *worth a visit for it contains relics from the Royal Charter and other local wrecks.* Continue past the current lifeboat station and along the shore edge to reach a memorial to the rescue of the crew of the *Hindlea* in 1959 from this headland. Follow the cliff-top path above Porth Helaeth. Later, after a footbridge, the path rises to a stone stile giving access to the Royal Charter monument. Afterwards continue with the cliff-top path to a good viewpoint across Porth Forllwyd and then on to pass a house. Continue along its access track. Before a large house turn RIGHT to follow the kissing gated path to another viewpoint overlooking Lligwy Bay. Continue along the cliffs to reach Traeth Lligwy car park.

2 From the car park follow the road past Dafarn Rhos to a junction. Keep ahead past Tyn Lon. Shortly, go through a kissing gate on the right signposted to Din Lligwy. *Nearby is the ruin of a 12thC Chapel of Ease.* Follow the waymarked path along field edges to two kissing gates and up through the trees to visit Din Lligwy. Afterwards, return to continue along the road – *enjoying extensive views east along the coast to the Great Orme and Snowdonia mountains.* Shortly a kissing gate gives access to Lligwy Neolithic burial chamber. *Built before 3000 BC, it contained the remains of 30 men, women and children. There is an illustration of how the massive 25 ton capstone may have been installed.* Continue along the road, then cross stiles on the left. Now follow the stiled path, later rising away from the stream, through several fields. After an enclosed path bear RIGHT past outbuildings and follow the driveway to a school. At the road beyond, follow it RIGHT back to the start.

WALK 23

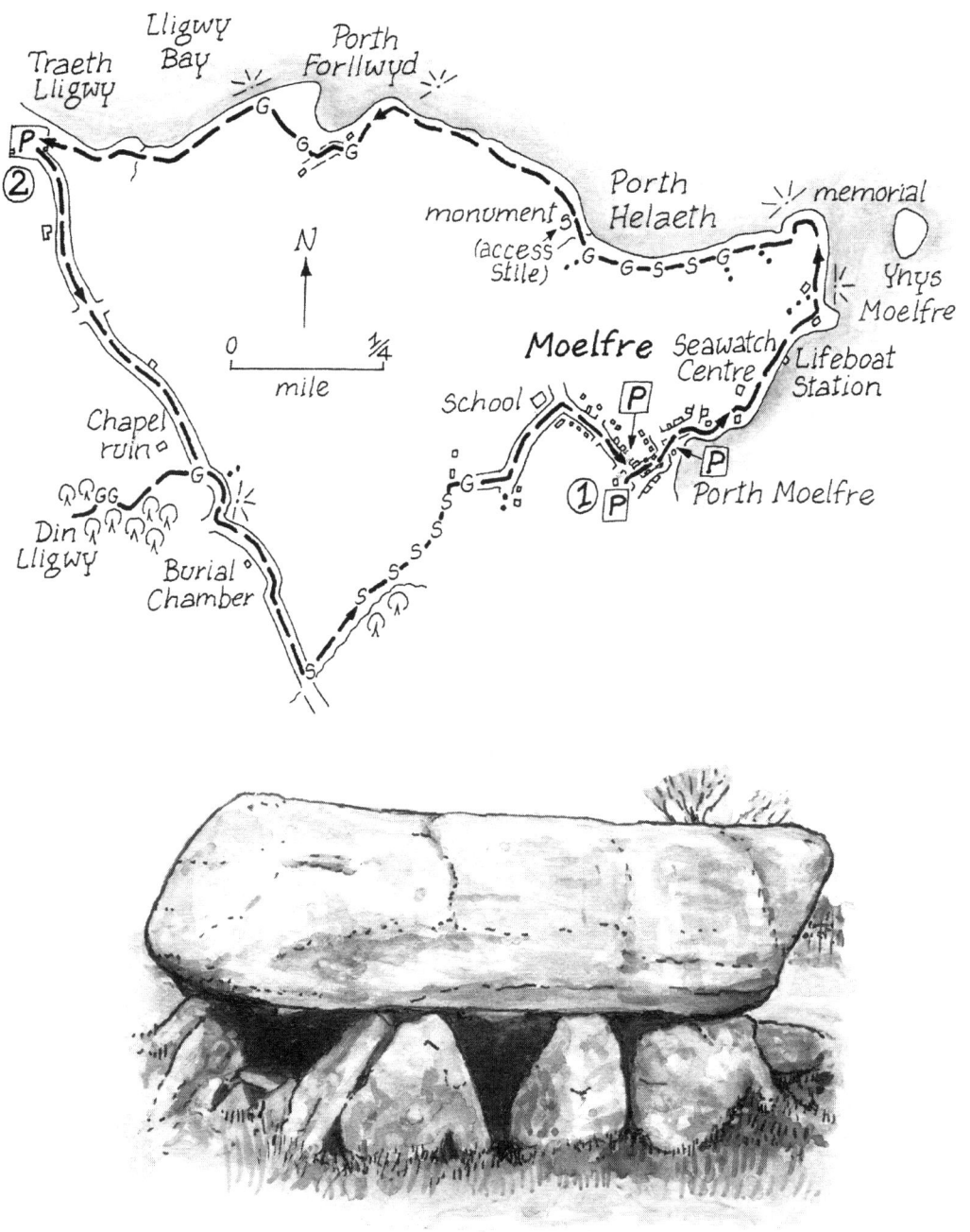

Neolithic burial chamber

WALK 24
MYNYDD CILAN

DESCRIPTION A delightful 3¾ mile (**A**) or 3¼ mile (**B**) walk around the attractive headland of Mynydd Cilan, part owned by the National Trust. The walk follows the waymarked Coast Path around the headland, returning by a choice of routes. **Walk A** continues on Coastal Path. **Walk B** completes the circuit of Open Access land. Allow about 2½ hours.
START Mynydd Cilan National Trust car park, Llŷn Peninsula [SH 295247].
DIRECTIONS From the main street in Abersoch follow the road to Sarn Bach, then continue with the road signposted to Cilan, later rising and passing an old chapel. Just past a no through road sign, turn right by Erw Deg bungalow along a lane which ends at cottages and the car park.

1 Follow the track past cottages, then take the right fork, soon descending. When it splits keep ahead. Just before a kissing gate, turn LEFT past Pen y Groes cottage and a ruin, then follow a rising green track ahead. Cross a track leading to Garreg Haul. At a waymark post turn RIGHT past a small lilly pond. Follow the path towards Porth Neigwl. At a waymark post turn LEFT along the wide headland path, soon bending left to a cross-road of paths. Here turn RIGHT past a waymark post. At a path junction just before a fence/embanked boundary, bear RIGHT to the boundary corner, then continue south up alongside the boundary and on to reach the trig point by a small underground reservoir. Continue on the delightful waymarked path, soon bending south-east along the headland, dipping then rising. At a waymark post at an old boundary corner, angle gently down to another post at the tip of the headland. Bear LEFT and follow a path up to a waymark post by an old iron gate – *offering a good view of Porth Ceiriad*.

2 Here you have a choice: For **Walk A**, turn RIGHT down the boundary to a kissing gate and go along the cliff edge to another kissing gate. After descending to a small gate, the path continues north between fences to a small gate. After a footbridge, it bends inland up to a kissing gate, then rises steadily to another kissing gate and continues up the field to go through a large wooden gate. Follow the boundary on your right up to a kissing gate. Go across the field to a kissing gate near Muriau, then follow its access track to the road. Follow it RIGHT, then at Erw Deg, follow the lane back to the start.

For **Walk B**, turn LEFT alongside the boundary, soon on a green track. Go past the boundary corner and a small reedy pool. When the track splits by a nearby small lake, keep ahead soon joining a track coming from the nearby white house. After 15 yards, take a path angling away on the right to go through a wide gap in the far boundary corner. Bear LEFT to follow an enclosed bridleway, soon becoming a track. Follow it past a house to eventually reach a track/lane junction near the start.

WALK 25
PORTH NEIGWL

DESCRIPTION A 3¾ mile (**A**) or 2¾ mile (**B**) low tide walk along the popular sandy beach at Porth Neigwl (Hell's Mouth), which has witnessed many shipwrecks, up onto the northern edge of Mynydd Cilan headland. It then follows paths inland to the ancient village of Llanengan, with its 15thC church and country inn. Allow about 2½ hours. The route can be combined with Walk 24 via a link path/track.
START Porth Neigwl National Trust car park, Llŷn Peninsula [SH 284267].
DIRECTIONS From Abersoch head to Llanengan and follow the road from the village to the car park.

1 Follow the path to the beach, then walk for ¾ mile towards Mynydd Cilan headland. (For **Walk B**, just before a stream, cross a stile on the top of the dunes, then follow a path over two further stiles, and across the next large field to cross a ladder-stile in the far right-hand corner. Turn left and

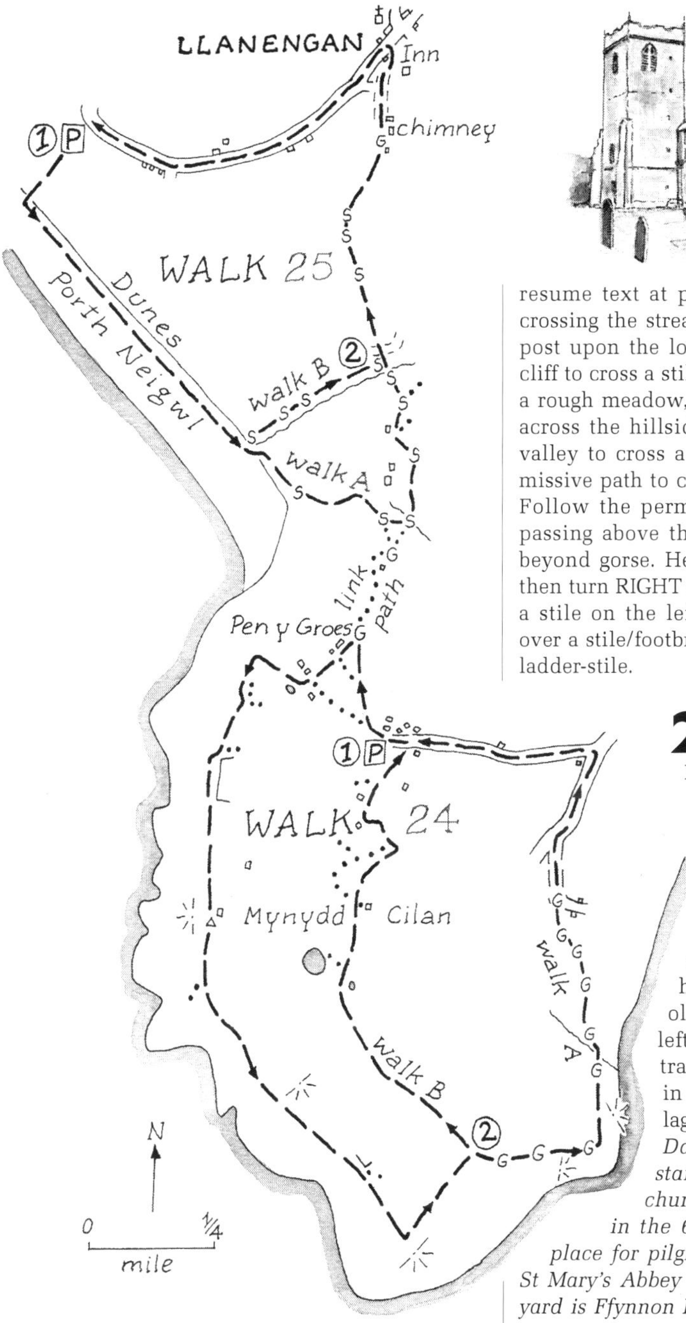

WALKS 24 & 25

St Engan's church

resume text at point **2**). For **Walk A**, after crossing the stream head over to a waymark post upon the low cliff. Continue along the cliff to cross a stile and go half-LEFT through a rough meadow, then follow a path angling across the hillside, soon bending along the valley to cross a stile. Bear LEFT on a permissive path to cross a stile, then footbridge. Follow the permissive path bearing LEFT, passing above the farm to cross a stile just beyond gorse. Head down towards a house, then turn RIGHT along the lower track. Cross a stile on the left, go along the field edge, over a stile/footbridge and past the adjoining ladder-stile.

2 Cross a track then follow the fence to a stile. Keep ahead to cross two further stiles, then follow the boundary towards a hilltop chimney – *that served a local lead-mine in the 19thC* – to go through an old gate by outbuildings. Follow the house's access track past old workings. When it bends left keep ahead along a shady track to reach the Sun Hotel in Llanengan. Go into the village to visit St Engan's church. *Dating from the 15thC, it stands on the site of an earlier church established by St Engan in the 6thC. It remains a popular place for pilgrimage in conjunction with St Mary's Abbey on Bardsey. In the churchyard is Ffynnon Engan, said to have healing properties.* Return to the Sun Hotel, perhaps for refreshments, then follow the road back to the start.

WALK 26
MYNYDD MAWR TO MYNYDD BYCHESTYN

DESCRIPTION An exhilarating undulating 4 mile circular walk linking two Open Access headlands at the end of the Llŷn peninsula, overlooking Bardsey island. The walk features dramatic cliff-top scenery, the departure point for pilgrims to Bardsey, historic St Mary's Well and great coastal views. Please take care as the cliff slopes are steep in places. *This walk is unsuitable for vertigo sufferers.* Allow about 2½ hours.
START Braich-y-Pwll, Uwchmynydd, Llŷn Peninsula. [SH 142256].
DIRECTIONS About 1 mile before Aberdaron, turn off the B4413 at a small hamlet, on a road signposted to Uwchmynydd. Follow the road through the scattered settlement of Uwchmynydd to enter National Trust Braich-y-Pwll after 2½ miles. Follow the lane to a grass parking area on the right opposite an information board.

For centuries, nearby Bardsey Island (Ynys Enlli), where St Mary's Abbey was established in the 13thC, has provided sanctuary for religious refugees, bards and pilgrims, many of whom chose to end their days there. Such was the religious importance of the island that it was said that three pilgrimages to Bardsey equalled one to Rome! From an inlet here, tradition says that in the Middle Ages thousands of pilgrims sailed across the treacherous Bardsey Sound. Nearby are ruins said to be of St Mary's church, where prayers were offered for a safe journey, and a spring in the rocks below high tide level, known as St Mary's Well, reputedly used by pilgrims before their dangerous journey. Until the Dissolution of the monasteries, much of the tip of the Llŷn was held by Bardsey Abbey. The island is now a National Nature Reserve run by the Bardsey Island Trust.

1 Go up the road and, just after it bends, head towards a seat above a small crag. Rejoin the single track road just beyond and follow it up to its end at the summit beneath the former coastguard hut, now an information centre. Return to the road end then follow a concrete path heading south towards Bardsey Island, later descending steps to a shelf containing the concrete foundations of several buildings. Descend to another green shelf below by a wide cleft in the ground. Descend to a further narrow green shelf 15 yards below, then follow a path down past an old spoil heap to reach a cross-path – *good views of the swirling currents below.* Turn LEFT and follow the faint path passing above a dramatic steep slope to the sea. When it splits keep with the lower fork, then when it starts bending left take a fainter path angling ahead down the slope. When it disappears head down the edge of the expansive grassy headland to pass a small crag to reach another lower down overlooking the sea.

2 Now head across open ground towards a distant small fenced enclosure on the lower slopes of Mynydd Gwyddel. As you are about to cross a small hollow just before reaching a stream, a path leads down to the sea above the western edge of the narrow rocky cove from where thousands of pilgrims reputedly sailed to Bardsey. A short scramble with care down the rock band brings you to just above the sea. To the right in the rock face is a tiny pool with water trickling down from a freshwater spring to the sea – St Mary's Well. Retrace your steps then cross the stream.

3 Now do a sharp u-turn aiming for the lower of two paths crossing the headland. The narrow path passes above the inlet, with Bardsey Island ahead, then follows the headland round to an optional route up a wide expanse. Continue on a path along the edge of the next rocky headland, then climb to its highest point. Now head inland across its craggy top, and follow a path down to level out below Mynydd Gwyddel, then descend to cross a ladder-stile below. Go along the clifftop, over another ladder-stile, then continue with the coastal path, later descending to cross two stiles.

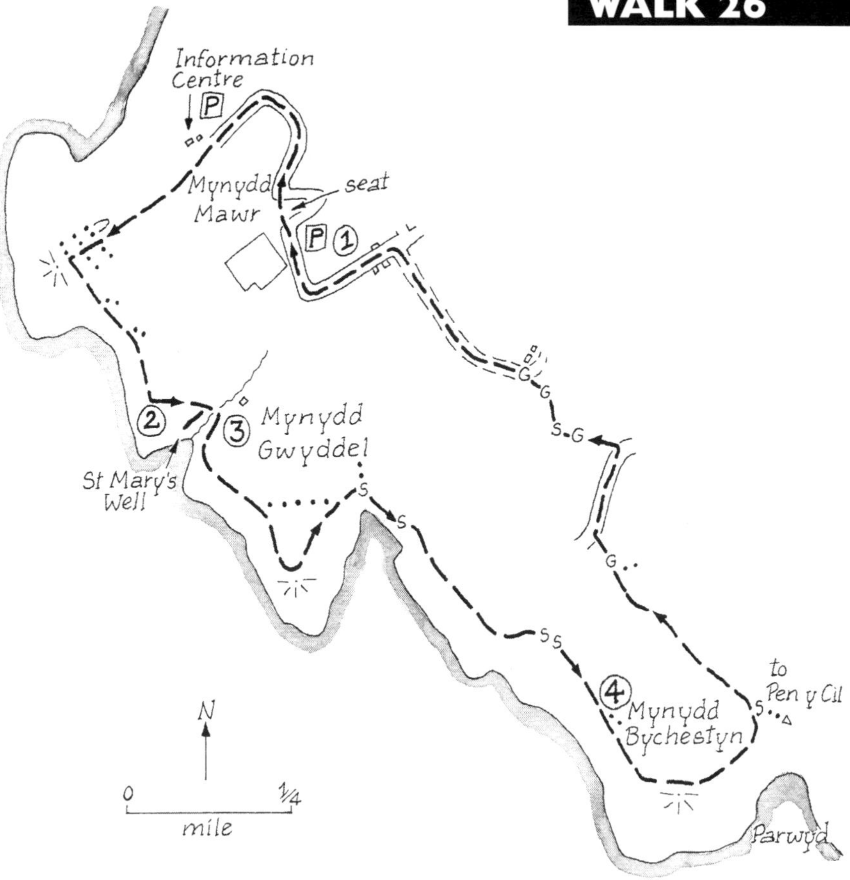

WALK 26

4 When it splits take the lower level fork. When it disappears head up to the nearby high ground to follow intermittent paths up to crags on the top of Mynydd Bychestyn. Follow a path above Parwyd inlet, with its massive 300 ft cliff face ahead, towards a fence. Follow the fence LEFT to a ladder-stile by a National Trust Bychestyn sign. (Here the walk can be extended to the nearby National Trust owned headland of Pen y Cil). Ignore the stile, but continue on a wide path alongside the fence to a gate and continue to a lane. Follow it RIGHT and on the bend take the signposted Coast Path along a track on the left. At its end follow the waymarked path through a facing gate and on over a ladder-stile. Go half-RIGHT across the field to cross a ladder-stile, then bear LEFT to go through a gateway near a large shed and follow the access track to the road. Follow it LEFT back to the start.

Bardsey

WALK 27
MYNYDD CARREG TO PORTH LLANLLAWEN

DESCRIPTION A 6½ mile (**A**) walk exploring an attractive section of the coast near the end of Llŷn linking varied National Trust land, and offering shorter 6 (**B**), 5½ (**C**), or 4¼ (**D**) walks. The route first visits a former lookout tower on the small hill of Mynydd Carreg, before following the delightful Coast Path to cross the western slopes of Mynydd Anelog, where there are a choice of routes. The main route **A**, for the more adventurous, continues across the more rugged slopes above the rocky inlet of Porth Llanllawen. The return route offers an opportunity for a short climb to the top of Mynydd Anelog (629 feet/192 metres) for great all-round views. Allow about 4 hours.
START National Trust Carreg car park, Llŷn Peninsula [SH 162290].
DIRECTIONS Near Pen-y-groeslon, 3½ miles from Aberdaron, turn off the B4413 on a road signposted to Porth Oer/Whistling Sands. After 2 miles, at a split turning on the right, keep ahead signposted to Aberdaron/Uwchmynydd, later passing the turning to Whistling Sands, then take the signposted Carreg car park turning on the right.

The information board reveals that Carreg (stone) takes its name from jasper, a semi-precious stone found locally and mined in the 18th and 19th centuries for decorative designs. The property was owned by the Carreg family from the 14thC until the mid-20thC.

1 Go through the kissing gate, then head RIGHT to another kissing gate and on up to the tower for good views of Whistling Sands. Return to the kissing gate then go half-RIGHT down the field to where you can see a fenced path below leading to the sea. Descend and go through a kissing gate and along the fenced path to another kissing gate to join the Coast Path. Turn LEFT. The path, marked by small waymark posts, meanders along the cliffs.

2 After ⅓ mile, at a waymark post just before the path bends into a small valley, turn away from the fence and descend to a National Trust sign just above a small cove. Here cross a stile and a new footbridge. The path rises steeply to a fence corner, then continues by the fence to another corner. It now rises and splits. Take the right fork past a path leading to a cottage to cross a ladder-stile. The delightful path now rises steadily up the heather/bracken covered hillside, later crossing a green track in a small depression, before rising to join a green track coming in from the left.

3 Shortly, when it splits near a small experimental enclosure, take the right fork. Keep up the main track past another enclosure onto a rise just beyond – *with a good view of Mynydd Anelog ahead.* Here divert to the right to a headland giving good views south to Mynydd Mawr. Return to the main track and follow it past your return side track (for **Walk D** turn left) and on alongside a wall/fence. At its corner, with a cottage to the left, go half-RIGHT to follow an intermittent path through bracken passing below a small enclosed spring. Soon the path becomes clearer, passes beneath a crag, then contours across the steep western slope of Mynydd Anelog, past a rising side path, before descending towards Porth Llanllawen to a stile in the boundary below by a coastal path waymark post.

4 Here you have a choice: (For **Walk C** follow a path left alongside the fence beneath Mynydd Anelog to join the return route. For **Walk B**, cross the stile and follow the waymarked path left, following the fence down to another stile. Head towards cottages to pass through a gate between outbuildings and another ahead on the right just before a house. Now follow its access track to reach a track coming in from the right at point **5**.)
For **Walk A**, continue ahead down the part bracken-covered slope, aiming for the fence

WALK 27

corner below, then follow the fence to a viewpoint overlooking Porth Llanllawen. Now work your way round just below the fence to pass above Porth Llanllawen, later descending a path to the National Trust. sign by a stream. Follow the stream up the valley, then cross a ladder-stile in the left-hand fence corner. Keep ahead, initially alongside the boundary, then continue across the field, angling to a fence corner ahead. Go alongside the boundary. In the corner, bear LEFT to the other corner and follow a path between boundaries, then bear RIGHT to go up a track to join another.

5 Go up the stony track, passing above a cottage. At a waymark post just before a farm, turn LEFT up a green track, then head to a ladder-stile ahead. Follow the boundary on the left towards a cottage. Cross its access track and follow a path beside the boundary up to a small gate back into National Trust land, where you are joined by **Walk C**.

Continue up the path by the boundary. At a post, take the left fork to pass behind a cottage. From here a short steep climb takes you to the top of Mynydd Anelog for extensive views. (Alternatively continue on the path along its lower slopes.) Continue along the ridge to a small cairn, then follow a descending path towards the sea, soon taking another path down to join the lower path just above the cottage. Follow it down to join your outward route at the wall corner. Continue down the green track.

6 Shortly, bear RIGHT down another track, soon bending LEFT besides a boundary, then continuing past the small enclosure to rejoin your outward route. Follow it down to the track junction, then take the right fork down past a cottage. After going through a gate, the path angles off the track past a pond and a building to go through a gate at the end of a stone barn. Follow the waymarked path along the field edge and through a gate. Keep ahead, go through a small gate and along a short path to the road. Follow it LEFT to a junction and back to the start.

WALK 28
MORFA NEFYN TO PORTH TOWYN

DESCRIPTION An exhilarating 8 mile linear walk via Porth Dinllaen following the cliff-top Coast Path along a splendid section of the rocky coastline linking two popular sandy bays, with seabirds and occasional seals for company for much of the way. With options for circular walks limited and a regular bus service available – no. 8 Pwllheli bus from Tudweiliog (daily services – visit: www.gwynedd.gov.uk/publictransport), this is the best way of enjoying this section of unspoilt coastline. Allow about 5 hours, plus sufficient time to walk ½ mile from Towyn farm to Tudweiliog for the bus.

START Car park at Towyn farm, Porth Towyn [SH 232374], or Tudweiliog, Llŷn Peninsula.

Walk start: Lon Golff, Morfa Nefyn SH 283405.

DIRECTIONS As you enter Tudweiliog from Nefyn on the B4417, take a minor road signposted to the beach for almost 1 mile to reach Towyn farm. At the end of outbuildings is a parking area kindly provided by the farmer. Note that this can quickly fill up in summer, so getting there in the morning is recommended.

Porth Dinllaen, protected by a long narrow headland, is the only good natural harbour on the northern coast of Llŷn, which was once a busy port, with over 600 vessels visiting a year by the end of the 18thC. During the early 19thC, there were serious proposals for it to be developed as the main port for Ireland, with a railway link to Bangor, but eventually Holyhead was chosen instead. The Ty Coch, built in 1823 as a vicarage, became an inn in 1842 to service workers in the shipbuilding yards on the beach. Overlooking Porth Dinllaen near the inn are the remains of an Iron Age coastal promontory fort.

1 Go through the farmyard and on along a wide hedge-lined gated track. A green track then continues up the field edge. After a small gate, go up the field edge to a kissing gate at a caravan site entrance. Follow the track up to the main road in Tudweiliog. Catch the bus at the PO/stores. At Morfa Nefyn it turns off the B4417 along Lon Las, and at cross-roads turns right. Alight at a bus stop 100 yards from the cross-roads (Rhos Bridin).

2 From the crossroads, go along Lon Golff to the golf club, then follow the lane down the golf course to a large building, where it becomes a stony track. (*If you wish to leave Porth Dinllaen for another time – turn left and follow a waymarked path across the golf link to Borth Wen.*) Continue along the track, soon forking down to Porth Dinllaen and the beach. If high tide return to the track and continue along the cliff-top to the lifeboat station. Otherwise go past the Ty

WALK 28

Coch inn and cottages to follow a path round the headland above the rocky shore past a cottage and on to the lifeboat station. From the top of its access track, go past the nearby mast and follow a path round the headland above the rocky shoreline, then climb up to pass to the left of a former lookout tower. Follow the path south along the western edge of the golf course overlooking the rocky coast, later bending above the shingly beach of Borth Wen. Continue with the waymarked path along the edge of the golf course.

Cwmistir – *look out for seals swimming in the clear turquoise sea* – then a Natural Arch. Distant caravans indicate your destination. Eventually you reach Porth Towyn and a seat overlooking the sandy beach makes a good finish. Even better if you have a picnic and beach gear in your car.

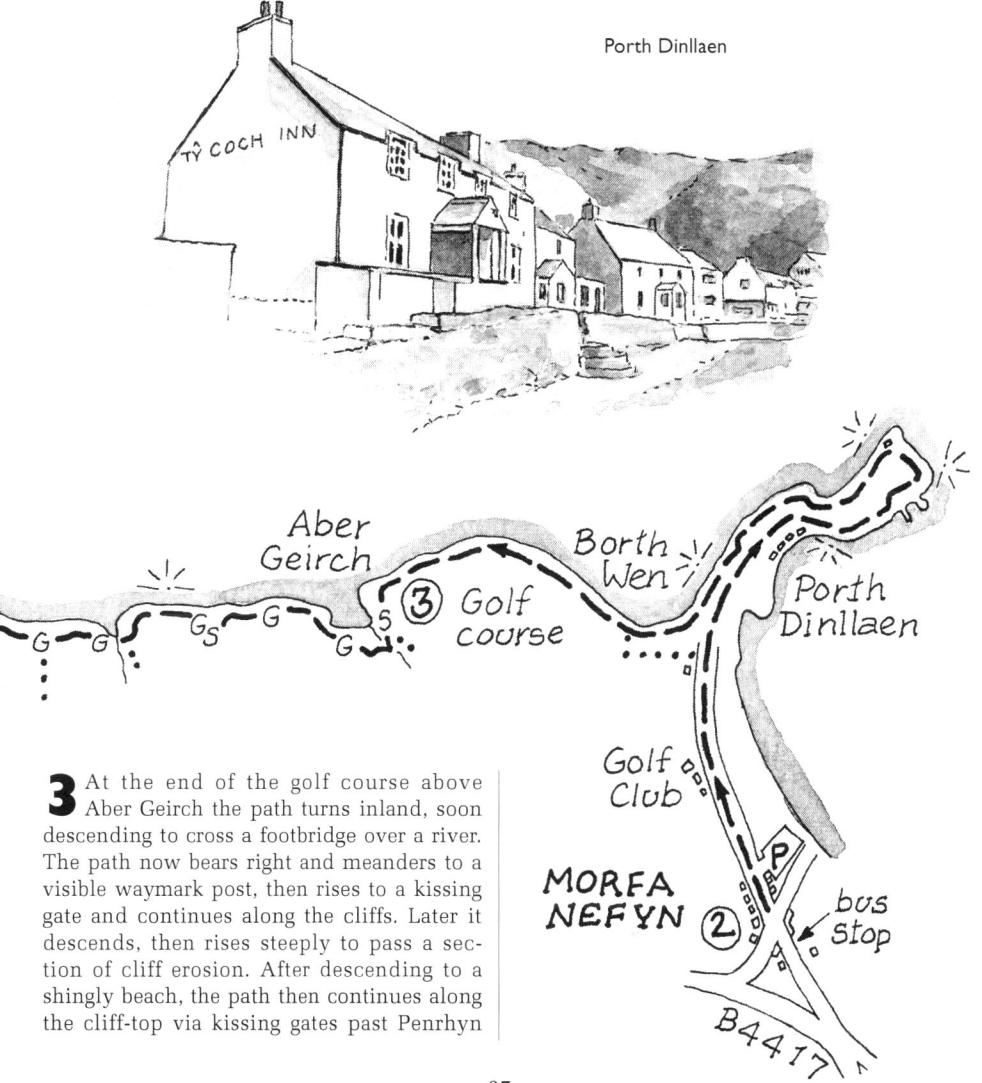

Porth Dinllaen

3 At the end of the golf course above Aber Geirch the path turns inland, soon descending to cross a footbridge over a river. The path now bears right and meanders to a visible waymark post, then rises to a kissing gate and continues along the cliffs. Later it descends, then rises steeply to pass a section of cliff erosion. After descending to a shingly beach, the path then continues along the cliff-top via kissing gates past Penrhyn

WALK 29
PISTYLL

DESCRIPTION A 2¾ mile walk exploring an attractive area of coastal land owned by the National Trust land, offering extensive views and the opportunity to visit a gem of a church. The route, which follows delightful paths guided by small waymark posts, first climbs across the higher ground, then descends to a viewpoint over Porth y Nant, before returning across a green shelf above Porth Pistyll for a final short climb. Allow about 2 hours.
START Pistyll National Trust car park., Llŷn [SH 330422].
DIRECTIONS Mid-way between Llithfaen and Nefyn, turn off the B4417 at Pistyll, on a minor road signposted St Beuno's Church, to the car park.

*S*t Beuno's *church is dedicated to the Celtic saint who founded a church here in the 6thC. This delightful simple church was an important place of worship for pilgrims on their way to Bardsey. The area later attracted many workers to quarry granite, which was shipped from a small port below Pistyll.*

I Go through the kissing gate and up the path. At a path junction keep ahead up to a viewpoint overlooking the church and along the coast. After a kissing gate continue ahead up the bracken/gorse covered hillside. At a stile bear LEFT up with the boundary then at its corner bear RIGHT. From the fence corner the path begins to rise, levels out and reaches a gate. Keep ahead across the bracken-covered hillside, later rising again – *with a view of Porth y Nant and Nant Gwrtheyrn.* The path now descends to a small gate and continues down to a wall. Here, turn LEFT. At the wall corner the path descends to join a cross-path.

2 Follow it RIGHT near the boundary to a stile overlooking Porth y Nant. Return to the path junction, then go down the wide path to a gate. The path descends further then levels out to go through a stock gate. The path continues across the lower bracken-covered slopes past meandering old walls. At a tall waymark post, first turn RIGHT through bracken to cross a stock gate. Go down the field edge to a kissing gate with a view overlooking the deep valley leading to Porth Pistyll. Return to the waymark post then follow the path angling up the hillside beneath old quarries, soon rising more steeply to join your outward route. Go through the kissing gate and follow the path down to the path junction. Bear RIGHT down to al ladder-stile onto the road. Follow it down to visit the delightful church.

St Bueno's church

WALKS 29 & 30

WALK 30
NANT GWRTHEYRN

DESCRIPTION A 3 mile walk featuring the dramatic setting of the former Porth y Nant quarry village, now restored as a residential Welsh Language Centre, interesting quarry remains and varying views throughout. The route descends into the steep enclosed valley by road or optional paths to Nant Gwrtheyrn, where a cafe provides refreshments. A path then descends to the shore, (from where there is a low tide beach option) before rising across bracken, then oak covered slopes, later returning by a bridleway. Allow about 2½ hours.

START Car Park by a forest above above Nant Gwrtheyrn, Llŷn Peninsula [SH 353441] reached from Lithfaen crossroads.

From the 1850s the area was transformed by the opening of three granite quarries to meet the demand for road-building material in the expanding cities of England, and the subsequent building of Porth y Nant village for the quarrymen and their families. The village, situated at the bottom of a steep enclosed valley above the sea, contained 24 houses, a foreman's house, co-op shop, bakery and chapel. All goods and materials for this isolated community were carried down on sledges. Quarrying ceased in the 1930s and the last family left in 1959. The village was later restored and residential Welsh courses have been held here since 1982, and a road has now considerably improved accessibility to the Centre.

1 From the information board, take the nearby signposted path into the forest, soon turning RIGHT down through the conifers to the road. Continue down the road. (After 100 yards is a path below on the right, which meanders down to briefly rejoin the road, before continuing after the bend on a forest track below the road, later rejoining it again.) The road passes a sharp bend at a prominent viewpoint, then continues down to eventually reach Nant Gwrtheyrn. Go past the former chapel, now the Heritage Centre, to visit Caffi Meinir.

2 Afterwards head towards the sea. After a gate the path descends towards the bottom of the long incline above the shore. When it splits beneath scree, go down the lower, initially stony path to just above the beach. (For a low tide option, go along the beach to its end by an old quarry, from where a track rises past cottages to point **3**.) Head to the incline, then the quarry's old winding equipment. Just beyond, take a waymarked path up across the bracken covered slopes, later crossing a stream. The path continues across Gallt y Bwlch, an area of small oak trees and an SSSI, before bending inland up towards Ciliau-isaf farm. At the wall go up steps, through a small gate, then pass above the farmhouse and follow its access track up to join another track.

3 Just before it meets the road, take a signposted bridleway through a small gate on the left, then go half-LEFT up a faint green track. When it fades follow the wall on your right up to an old iron ladder-stile, then up to a small gate – *enjoying extensive views*. Go half-LEFT up the waymarked path – *with Yr Eifl ahead*. After a gate, continue ahead up near the old boundary, then after 100 yards bear RIGHT up across a small top and on towards a cottage to go through a gate in the boundary corner ahead. Follow the boundary on your left through two fields (gates) then continue to the road and the start.

PRONUNCIATION

Welsh	English equivalent
c	always hard, as in **c**at
ch	as in the Scottish word lo**ch**
dd	as th in **th**en
f	as f in o**f**
ff	as ff in o**ff**
g	always hard as in **g**ot
ll	no real equivalent. It is like 'th' in then, but with an 'L' sound added to it, giving 'thlan' for the pronunciation of the Welsh 'Llan'.

In Welsh the accent usually falls on the last-but-one syllable of a word.

KEY TO THE MAPS

- ⟶ Walk route and direction
- ═ Metalled road
- --- Unsurfaced road
- •••• Footpath/route adjoining walk route
- ∼ River/stream
- ♣♧ Trees
- ▬▬ Railway
- **G** Gate
- **S** Stile
- **F.B.** Footbridge
- Viewpoint
- **P** Parking
- **T** Telephone

THE COUNTRYSIDE CODE

- Be safe – plan ahead and follow any signs
- Leave gates and property as you find them
- Protect plants and animals, and take your litter home
- Keep dogs under close control
- Consider other people

Open Access
Some routes cross areas of land where walkers have the legal right of access under The CRoW Act 2000 introduced in May 2005. Access can be subject to restrictions and closure for land management or safety reasons for up to 28 days a year. Please respect any notices. The Countryside Council for Wales website (www.ccw.gov.uk) provides updated information on any closures.

About the author, David Berry

David is an experienced walker with a love of the countryside and an interest in local history. He is the author of a series of walks guidebooks covering North Wales, where he has lived and worked for many years, and been a freelance writer for Walking Wales magazine. He has also worked as a Rights of Way surveyor across North Wales and served as a member of Denbighshire Local Access Forum. For more information visit: www.davidberrywalks.co.uk

Published by **Kittiwake-Books Limited**
3 Glantwymyn Village Workshops, Glantwymyn, Machynlleth, Montgomeryshire SY20 8LY

© Text & map research: David Berry 2012
© Maps & illustrations: Kittiwake-Books Ltd 2012
Drawings by Morag Perrott
Cover photos: Main: Ynys Llanddwyn, Anglesey (Walk 12). *Inset:* Llandudno Pier (Walks 5 & 6). David Berry

Care has been taken to be accurate. However neither the author nor the publisher can accept responsibility for any errors which may appear, or their consequences. If you are in any doubt about access, check before you proceed.

Printed by MWL, Pontypool.

ISBN: **978 1 908748 04 1**